THE USES OF TELEVISION IN AMERICAN HIGHER EDUCATION

The Uses of Television in American Higher Education

James Zigerell

PRAEGER

New York
Westport, Connecticut
London

To Rosamond

Library of Congress Cataloging-in-Publication Data

Zigerell, James.
    The uses of television in American higher education / James
Zigerell.
       p.   c m.
    Includes bibliographical references and index.
    ISBN 0-275-93318-0
    1. Television in higher education—United States. 2. Distance
education—United States. I. Title.
LC6576.Z54   1991
378.1'7358'0973—dc20   90-36600

British Library Cataloguing in Publication Data is available.

Library of Congress Catalog Card Number: 90-36600
ISBN: 0-275-93318-0

First published in 1991

Praeger Publishers, One Madison Avenue, New York, NY 10010
An imprint of Greenwood Publishing Group, Inc.

Printed in the United States of America

The paper used in this book complies with the
Permanent Paper Standard issued by the National
Information Standards Organization (Z39.48–1984).

10 9 8 7 6 5 4 3 2 1

Contents

Introduction:
A Rocky Road to Acceptance

Some readers of this book may find it difficult to imagine a world without television. Television, nonetheless, has been with us only for a short time — that is, short as historians reckon time. Yet some readers cannot remember a time when television was not part of daily life. For most Americans, it is now the primary source of their entertainment, provided conveniently in their own homes off the air waves or in videocassette recordings. For many, the TV set has displaced the daily newspaper as the source of information as to happenings around the world and in their own communities.

What is remarkable about the medium is its omnipresence. Sports fans sitting in arenas where the games are actually being played carry with them small TV sets and divide their attention between the TV screen and the live action. Shoppers in supermarkets watch videotapes demonstrating the care and preparation of fresh fruits and vegetables. Some shoppers are even deserting the malls and the stores, and are telephoning in orders as they see merchandise displayed on their TV sets at home.

However, television is not all entertainment or merchandising. Lawyers, accountants, nurses, and sales people gather in hotel meeting rooms or in hospital lounges and offices to watch television and brief themselves on recent changes in legislation and tax laws, or in new clinical and surgical procedures. Businessmen gather at local chambers of commerce to be updated by satellite on recent developments in Washington, D.C., concerning legislative issues relevant to their interests. Thus, it is easy to be infected by the enthusiasm of promoters and zealots and believe that the video media, along with telecommunications media like the computer, are certain not only to change all aspects of our lives — work, leisure, education, health care — but also to transform completely our social relationships. One observer, in a popular book, has dubbed our society "The Wired Society."[1]

RECOGNIZING THE EDUCATIONAL POTENTIAL OF THE MEDIUM

The potential and promise of the video medium for disseminating instruction at all levels were recognized by educators early in the television age — as was radio's same potential early in the radio age. In retrospect, we can see that television could not have appeared at a more propitious time for higher education. When World War II ended, higher education in the United States entered a period of tremendous strain and growth. Hundreds of thousands of men and women returned from military service to civilian life entitled to the generous educational benefits of the historic G.I. Bill. These, along with the many young Americans who were not old enough for military service coming out of high school, put heavy pressures on the physical plants and faculty resources of colleges and universities. In a few years, too, the impact of the postwar baby boom was to be felt.

Then, too, educators were feeling concern about the many older adults who wanted to enroll part-time in colleges during evening hours. With the flood of students of conventional college age spilling over into the late afternoon and evening hours, how could all those adults, of whom most were employed during the day, be adequately served? Exacerbating the problem even more was a remarkable social phenomenon. Since World War II, growing egalitarian feelings, present not only in the United States but throughout the world, were creating strong demands for educational opportunities for all adults, no matter what their status in life. Eventually, the celebrated British Open University (BOU), which extensively employs the electronic media — radio, television, the computer, and still other devices — dramatically embodied one response to this demand. By so doing, as we shall see, it stands as, perhaps, the greatest educational achievement of the twentieth century.

Another response, of course, was to expand higher education facilities and build new institutions all over the country. This happened during the 1960s when it was said a new two-year community college was opening every week. Still another and less costly response was to maximize already existing resources. Here television and the burgeoning TV technologies seemed a godsend.

Unfortunately, some years after the events, we are forced to conclude that at times television may very well have been pressed into the service of higher education for the wrong reasons. During the late 1950s and early 1960s, the enrollment boom years, academic departments and administrators saw television merely as a way to contain the flood of students. Scarce faculty resources could be conserved and specialists freed to teach advanced classes if undergraduate students watched closed-circuit TV lectures in classrooms and auditoriums. Sometimes, the students watched all alone. At other times, they watched under the supervision of graduate assistants. Some schools even had graduate assistants meet with them in tutorial sessions.

However, in 1952, when the Federal Communications Commission set aside 242 TV channels for noncommercial uses (80 in the VHF range — that is, channels 2 through 13 — and the others on UHF, channel 14 and higher), adult educators in particular saw in these channels valuable ways of distributing instruction off campus. University of Houston administrators, for example, recognized these reserved channels as arms whereby instruction could be extended while at the same time relieving them of the need for construction. They built noncommercial station KUHT to send lectures out to students in a variety of locations: in their homes, in university dormitories, in special TV viewing areas. Eric Barnow, historian of broadcasting in the United States, supplies an accurate assessment of such experiences: "Lectures-by-television were probably no worse than in large halls — in some ways undoubtedly better. But KUHT's successions of lectures was hardly a beacon light for non-commercial television."[2]

Excitement as to the promise of television for education was further fueled by the zeal of a new breed of specialists called educational technologists. They began to appear in numbers in schools and on college campuses in the late 1950s and 1960s. The following excerpt from a 1962 study supported by what was then still known as the U.S. Office of Education shows the euphoric feelings television and the communications media inspired in some educators:

The advent of television . . . has given Americans unparalleled opportunities to advance in the ability to record and communicate ideas. These new communications resources must now be harnessed to serve the ends of education when American school and college programs must now find new and improved ways to cope with spiraling enrollments and increasing shortages of adequate classrooms and able teachers. . . .

These new technologists are not just the familiar audiovisualists with their movie and slide projectors. Rather, they claim to be instrumental in reshaping instruction itself and in reaching new audiences for formal and informal instruction. The study just cited ends with this ringing statement: "The new media and devices now available to education hold as much promise for improvement of instruction as did the invention of the book."[3]

References to the new media, especially video, as having the impact on our society Gutenberg's press had on sixteenth-century society were heard more and more as Marshall McLuhan's often murky pronouncements on the media caught the attention of the public in the 1960s and 1970s.

In actual fact, the progress of instructional TV usage in the United States since the 1950s can be described as a series of sharp peaks and valleys. Yet, despite frustrated hopes and frequent disappointments, ITV managed to survive the rash promises made by its glib promoters and mindless enthusiasts, as well as the costly experiments that came to nothing. In spite of imprudent employment of the medium and persistent failures to take advantage of its distinctive presentational properties, it has made, and continues to make, a place for itself, humble and still marginal though it may be, in the world of higher education. Few doubt nowadays that "television works as an educational tool," in the words of *Learning by Television,* an influential 1966 report on instructional television commissioned by the Ford Foundation, one of its most loyal and munificent supporters in its early years.[4] Even though instructional TV producers were being regularly reviled for filling screens with professorial "talking faces" flanked by chalkboards, still an education writer for *Time* could comment: ". . . not only is a taped professor as informative as a live one, but he seldom turns sour and never grows weary of talking." In short, his conclusion was that "despite . . . resistance, proof of television's viability shows up in almost every study of its effectiveness."[5]

Short-lived as some of the country's well-funded college-level instructional TV projects were, the medium has still managed to secure its place in higher education, especially as need for and interest in distance teaching and learning has grown. In part, this book is intended to describe this interest. A 1988 issue of *Business Week* carried a feature article on media-based distance teaching and learning. The article in question quotes a former Federal Communications Commission member as saying that "the electronic college is finally emerging."[6]

The interest of a journal like *Business Week* is indicative of another reason for television's increasing acceptance as an instructional tool. Training and education are no longer exclusive domains of the schools and colleges. Any reasonably well-informed citizen is aware that wrenching socioeconomic changes are currently taking place within American society. These changes are necessitating vast programs of training and retraining that the schools and colleges cannot provide on their own — even if all of them were willing to do so. Thousands of aliens from non-European cultures and societies must be integrated into our way of life. Currently, accelerating shifts from an industrial economy to one tied to high technology and services, rather than to materials production, are leaving many adults in mid-life with obsolete job skills or skills only in limited demand. The private sector, both business and industrial, is now investing, and will invest even more, in training workers outside the normal school setting. Television will be employed for much of this training.

Needs Served by Television

Lord Walter Perry, operational head of the BOU during its opening and formative years, called the world's attention to the insistent public demand in the latter part of this century for a product — education — and the fortuitously converging means of delivering the product at reasonable cost to those demanding it at their convenience through the electronic media.[7] This convergence of demand and the means of supplying it was a lucky stroke for a developed nation like the United Kingdom, where a frankly elitist system traditionally excluded the mass of the people from higher education. It has also proved to be fortunate for developing nations, in Asia and elsewhere, where expanding whatever higher education structure was in place would have been a prohibitively expensive and prolonged process.

To their credit, planners at organizations like UNESCO were quick to recognize the potential of television in attacking the urgent educational problems of the world's developing countries. They saw the following as needs television was well able to serve:

1. The need for improving instruction in the classroom;
2. The need to teach those who will themselves be teachers of the young and old;
3. The need to spread literacy and the skills required to live in an urban technological society;
4. The need to provide continuing education for adults;
5. The need to provide extramural extensions of the school and college.[8]

All of these needs, except for the second, are of immediate interest to anyone concerned with adult and continuing education; the second addresses the professional development needs of teachers; the third relates to problems of combatting illiteracy among adults and teaching the skills that people recently arrived in our cities need to cope with urban life; both four and five address the demand for extending instruction beyond the walls of the classroom into homes and community centers at times convenient for adults. These are the very needs that prompted the Ford Foundation, that twentieth-century Maecenas, to invest more than $10 million so as to encourage instructional uses of television from the elementary school up to the university.

The first of the needs listed above is still of great interest to proponents of TV instruction at all levels, since they cling to the hope that elementary school teachers as well as university lecturers may model their own teaching techniques on those of the skilled teachers they see on television. In 1958, for instance, the National Broadcasting Company, with the financial support of the Ford Foundation, started a short-lived project featuring "master" teachers on open TV broadcast. *Continental Classroom,* as it was aptly called, recruited as hosts professors noted both for their mastery of their subjects and their presentational skills. The project was designed to provide college-level courses people could watch on television in their homes and models of the art of teaching for teachers across the country to watch. Can anyone doubt that teachers can learn about teaching their subject matters from observing effective TV teachers? Unfortunately, this is a difficult outcome to measure, especially at the college and university level where professional esteem is often prickly.

Focus of This Book

The purpose of this study is to acquaint a reader interested in instructional television, as well as a general reader interested in problems of education, with the uses to which the medium has and is being put by U.S. colleges and universities. It does not pretend to be a history of instructional television in U.S. higher education, although it does rest on a roughly historical framework.

Above all, it is not intended in any sense to be a survey of the video technologies now being employed in colleges and universities. Manuals that do this are readily available.[9] The author is not a technologist by training or by inclination. His principal, almost sole, interest is in the uses to which the video technologies are being put in instruction.

The opening sections will describe the audiences for instructional television — that is, the kinds of people who are learning via television — as well as the attitudes and concerns of faculties. These chapters will also discuss instructional TV design and production. Succeeding chapters will review efforts made to evaluate the effectiveness of television instruction and the characteristics of television learners. Attention will also be devoted to the impact of television on the currently flourishing distance learning movement. Some attention will be paid to the fruitful interinstitutional and cooperative relationships that have grown out of expanding uses of television in postsecondary education and training. We shall consider, too, the impact of newer video technologies on college-level instruction, although as just noted, our interest will not be in the technologies, their technical capabilities, or specifications, but in how they can help educators serve people in new ways. In short, if the author can persuade the reader that instructional television, though far from being in the mainstream, is an increasingly important arm of U.S. higher education, he will have fulfilled his purpose.

Making the Walls Fall

DELIVERING INSTRUCTION TO
NEW KINDS OF LEARNERS

Adult educators the world over, as stated in the introduction, were not slow to recognize the instructional potential of broadcast media, first radio and later television, for extending instruction to people in their homes and other places outside the school room. In the early days of radio broadcast, as long ago as 1926, the British Broadcasting Corporation had a proposal for a "wireless university." In 1927, the BBC already had an adult education division.[1] American educators also saw radio as an adjunct of adult education. Some of the earliest radio stations were even under university control. The University of Wisconsin, always a leader in extension education, had its own educational radio station, WHA, in operation as early as 1919. The historians of radio as an educational tool remind us that "there were some significant achievements during these years that demonstrated the medium's [radio's] potential."[2]

As was only to be expected, with its powerful sensory impact and its remarkable powers of dissemination, television was recognized immediately as an instructional tool of the greatest value. Indeed, the first use of television for instruction occurred before what we think of as the age of television. In 1933, the State University of Iowa telecast a violin recital, a discussion, and a sketching lesson. Fifteen years later in 1948, when the new medium had achieved viability and commercial television was beginning its conquest of the country's leisure time, some eight colleges and universities were presenting educational programs on television.

Fortunately, before it was too late, the Federal Communications Commission came to the assistance of the educational community and blunted somewhat the rapacity of the commercial interests. As has already been noted, in 1952 a band of license assignments was set aside for noncommercial users. The result of this, which came about through the tireless efforts of dedicated educators and public-spirited citizens, was Educational, or, as it is now known, Public Television, established to give the general public an alternative to the programming on commercial television.

The picture, at first, was not a rosy one for educators. Most of the channels allocated were in the UHF range at a time when most TV sets received UHF signals poorly. From the very beginning, for that matter, educational broadcasters have had trouble finding facilities and times to air their products. Open air time for colleges and universities, whether on VHF or UHF, grows ever scarcer and in the major broadcast markets, where it is still sometimes available from public broadcast stations, it becomes more and more expensive for colleges to lease. When time is available, it is often scheduled when it is inconvenient for adult viewers with work and family responsibilities to watch. The new television technologies introduced in recent years, however — cable television, satellite communications, microwave transmission, and home videocassette players — are now relieving some of these difficulties for colleges and universities looking for ways to deliver video-based instruction.

Attitudes Toward Instructional Television

The problem of access to broadcast facilities, seemingly intractable though it can be, has never been so knotty a one as that posed by skeptical, and at times even intransigent, faculty members and administrators on campuses. This kind of resistance to change explains the frequency of missed opportunities in higher education. Why, one wonders, has radio played so slight a part in extending higher education in this country? As one observer notes, educational radio was never more than an "experiment." The reason for its failure "was the lack of commitment by educational leaders to developing the medium for instructional purposes."[3] Herein lies a great irony, for there never really has been any doubt as to the effectiveness of either radio or television for instruction. The real challenge on college campuses has been to find rightful places for these media. The Carnegie Commission on the Future of Public Broadcasting summed the issue up well in a 1979 report. They concluded that the question is not "whether television and radio can teach, but how they can be best used for learning."[4]

Even though television has been employed for college-level instruction for over thirty years, except in the community colleges, faculties and administrators have not addressed the Carnegie Commission challenge just quoted. One reason, of course, is that the matter is of only marginal concern on most college campuses. Another is that extension education, whether it be conducted in conventional ways or by way of video, radio, or computers, is not a matter of consuming interest to faculties. Still another is that university faculties tend to resent suggestions as to how they can improve or enrich their teaching.

As a result, there has been no vigorous discussion, except by those with a vested interest, of how video can be most effectively employed to supplement conventional classroom instruction, or how, or whether, it can be used effectively as a surrogate for classroom instruction. At best we hear uttered on campuses hopes that echo the pious recommendations of the Carnegie Commission report. Can these capabilities of video be better employed to supplement classroom instruction, or should they be used as a surrogate for conventional classroom instruction? The Carnegie report, which we shall be referring to again, urged among other recommendations that public broadcasters and federal agencies "support the research necessary to identify and develop the capabilities of . . . television for learning."[5]

Initial Acceptance

If we were to trace the growth and acceptance of instructional TV, we would trace a curve moving downward from early and enthusiastic support in some quarters in the 1950s to the real disenchantment that set in during the 1960s. Definite movement upward did not start again until the end of the 1960s and the beginning of the 1970s. It was prompted by the success of the British Open University and a spate of efforts in this country to adapt or imitate it — efforts which proved futile and short-lived.

Since the 1970s, too, increasing sophistication in instructional TV design and production has persuaded more and more people that television can indeed represent a satisfying kind of instruction for adults learning on their own. The one TV series that inspired belief that television with broad appeal could "educate" was not a college-credit course but the hugely successful and still celebrated *Sesame Street*, which first appeared on Public Broadcast stations in 1968. The compilers of the Carnegie Commission's *A Public Trust*, cited above, noted: "Before *Sesame Street*, most educational television programs involved inexpensive production techniques, talking heads, and little imagination." The Commission concluded that, in this project, "For the first time, educational researchers and professional producers worked closely together in creating a television series that was both instructive and entertaining."[6] *Sesame Street* and its producers, The Children's Television Workshop, received financial support from the U.S. Office of Education and the Corporation for Public Broadcasting. The history of educational television, that is, of television with instruction as one of its primary goals, can be divided handily into pre– and post–*Sesame Street* periods.

Uncertainty as to Goals

Attentive readers — suspicious might be perhaps a more accurate term — may have detected a note of uncertainty in the last sentence as to whether television programming of the *Sesame Street* kind should be called "educational" or "instructional." Unfortunately, this uncertainty, or confusion, exists in the public mind, and has, it can be argued, hindered the development of instructional television in this country. The lack of definition of "educational" in television programming allows public broadcasters, whenever they are criticized for not airing enough really educational/instructional programs, to respond that their responsibility is to give American audiences an alternative to the program fare served up by the commercial broadcasters. No one can deny that a telecast, say, of a play by Henrik Ibsen or Anton Chekhov is educational in a broad and real sense. However, as some public broadcasters do, can we stretch education to cover the stream of second-rate movies and popular entertainment offered too often on some PBS stations? Such a programming policy, in the opinion of some observers, threatens to convert the public broadcasting service into just another entertainment network.

The recommendations of an earlier Carnegie Foundation–supported report on educational television, *Public Television: A Program for Action*, which resulted in the passage by Congress of the Public

Broadcast Act of 1967, knowingly or unknowingly led to making educational broadcast less instructional and more entertaining. This commission strove to reconcile sets of conflicting interests, among them "the interests of those who advocated centering noncommercial television in instruction and education and those who advocated a broader public service role." By replacing educational television (ETV) with public television (PTV) they intended to emphasize "programming for general enrichment and information, as well as for classroom instruction."[7]

It is understandable that anyone trained in television production methods suspects that an educator employing television perceives the medium as simply a way of transmitting talking images of tweedy professors anchored to lecterns, turning occasionally to blackboards for visual variety. The professional broadcaster takes a different view of the medium, approaching the instructional TV program as a distinctive kind of experience that can be incorporated into a larger educational scheme.

These opposing points of view, as exaggerated as the opposition admittedly is, point to a persistent problem in the world of instructional television, one we shall have occasion to return to later. Can the demands of direct instruction be reconciled with those of mass media entertainment? A teacher is concerned with television as a means of imparting formal instruction, the student's mastery of which is measured in end-of-term examinations and the like. This kind of television seldom attracts audiences large enough to warrant a professional broadcaster's attention. On the other hand, some educators and public figures — adult educators in particular — like to think there are, by their standards at least, vast audiences reachable via this new medium.

Thus, utopian educational dreams were sparked anew. For example, a retired World War II general saw possibilities for national town meetings, with the president of the United States reporting to the people, and the people responding via electronic devices.[8] Ideas were advanced for courses in American history presented on television by noted historians, adult educators, and prominent public figures. The success of cultural performances on PBS only fanned these hopes. Several million viewers would view one televised performance of *Hamlet,* more spectators than perhaps watched the tragedy unfold in all its stage performances since its composition. Audience surveys estimate that 5 percent of American households viewed a televised performance of Puccini's *La Boheme* from New York City's Lincoln Center on one evening in 1977.

Sadly, the audiences that instructional broadcasters found sometimes become impatient with them. Even though they lacked both the financial and the professional resources for lively TV production, their audiences still expected it of them. A whole generation had grown to maturity since television had invaded American life. One thing can certainly be said of commercial television: it may be short on substance, but it is seldom short on slickness and pace. As a result, only audiences with specialized interests will tolerate what most consider the dullness of instructional television.

EARLY FAILURES AND SUCCESSES

It has already been noted that several universities experimented with television in its primordial days, but it was not until the late 1940s and the early 1950s that television began to display its educational potential. The University of Michigan was employing it for adult education in 1948. In 1953, American University in Washington, D.C., was using the medium. As already noted, once the FCC had set aside channels dedicated to noncommercial use, the University of Houston began operating the first ETV station. The University of Nebraska was also involved in TV instruction early, and has continued as a major production house and the center of a statewide network through its television station.

No useful purpose would be served by listing all the colleges and universities involved. However, the University of North Carolina at Chapel Hill deserves special mention, because it soon became the center of a notable state educational network and a leader in offering continuing education to people of its state. As still other universities acquired noncommercial television licenses, they began to offer college-level courses to adult viewers, although often only fitfully.

Closed-Circuit Television (CCTV) Teaching

Besides those who attempted open-broadcast, there were institutions that turned to closed-circuit, or in-house, television, as soon as this technology was available. Such systems carry television signals by cable from one location to another within the institution itself or from one campus to another. As new colleges were constructed and existing ones expanded, and when grant money for television and telecommunications equipment was liberally dispensed by federal and state government sources in the 1960s and 1970s, closed-circuit television installations and TV production studios became commonplace on U.S. campuses.

Among the larger state universities, Michigan State University was offering courses on closed circuit by the early 1950s. The students watched TV monitors in classrooms, in student centers — even in their dormitories. By 1973, about the time that college and university interest in uses of closed circuit on campus was waning, the 11-channel Michigan State system had carried as many as 324 courses, in which students had earned some 57,000 credit hours.[9]

One closed-circuit project in particular deserves special notice, if only because it received such wide publicity. Pennsylvania State University introduced its CCTV instructional system in 1952. The system attracted much attention both in this country and abroad during the later 1950s and early 1960s, and was emulated by other colleges and universities. As was indicated above, during the 1960s state and federal agencies made funds available for closed-circuit installations on campuses. Hopes were running high not only that CCTV would help alleviate the post–World War II teacher shortage, but also that it would relieve the pressures on academic departments by freeing staff members from the onerous load of teaching mostly introductory-level courses. Offering high-enrollment introductory and required courses on closed circuit would release senior staff for more advanced and specialized teaching and spare them the drudgery of helping teach multisection courses in their disciplines.

The beguiling belief was that large-enrollment classes — beginning chemistry and physics, introductory psychology, economics — could be presented effectively on closed-circuit television by skilled instructors with some minimal TV production assistance. Pictures could be sent out to 1,000 students watching in various locations. The programs, once videotaping equipment was on the market at reasonable cost, were also to be recorded for later use.

Some colleges, unlikely as it seems in retrospect, were even established as television and media-based teaching institutions. The University of Toronto's Scarborough College, when it was founded, employed television lectures for its undergraduate instruction.[10] Florida Atlantic University was established on a similar premise. Both experiments came about in response to fears that student enrollments on campuses would continue to explode throughout the 1960s. Both, however, failed ingloriously. Whether or not faculty or students were well enough prepared for the innovation, neither accepted it and both institutions reverted to conventional methods of instruction. All in all, the innovators did not reckon with the strength of faculty hostility, the extent of student dissatisfaction, and the shock of radical change.

When inexpensive videotape became available in the 1960s, the Pennsylvania State CCTV system was expanded into a full-blown educational TV facility to serve the entire state. In fact, campus closed-circuit systems that survived soon were being linked so as to serve larger areas — entire counties, for example. The State of South Carolina's statewide linkage, an admirable example of such networks, now makes it possible for remote, or distant, learners to watch lectures at sites throughout the state and earn graduate degrees from the state university. These same learners, of course, are required to submit correspondence exercises, attend sessions on campus periodically, and take examinations. They satisfy, in effect, whatever is demanded of students who complete degrees in the conventional way. Other states — Indiana is a good example — have likewise linked campuses of their public colleges and universities electronically to encourage resource sharing, and, as legislators and tax-payers always hope, to discourage costly duplication of facilities — and faculties.

The Pennsylvania State CCTV systems, perhaps, raised the highest hopes of all such projects. As indicated above, Pennsylvania State received major funding from the Ford Foundation and was expected to become a model of its kind. Elaborate studies of the project were undertaken by the Foundation, ranging from assessments of student attitudes toward televised instruction in the classroom to comparisons of the performance of students receiving televised instruction with that of students receiving conventional instruction.

The authors of the already cited and widely discussed 1966 assessment of Ford Foundation–supported instructional TV projects, *Learning by Television,* judged the Pennsylvania State project to be successful on the whole, but their total evaluation was far from a ringing endorsement. It was not, as already stated, so widely imitated as its supporters anticipated, and it encountered dogged faculty resistance. Yearly enrollments in the CCTV courses went as high as 20,000 by 1962, but leveled off to about 13,000 in later years. Although the courses were usually offered live on the Pennsylvania State campus, other colleges and universities did use some courses in recording.[11]

Unfortunately for its champions, student and faculty response to closed-circuit television was generally not favorable. This attitude became apparent as long ago as 1965 in the results of a student attitudes survey commissioned by the Ford Foundation and reported in *Learning by Television.* Students complained regularly about lack of personal contact with their teachers. Not surprisingly, they deplored the lack of video production finesse and the prevailing dullness of the lectures. This was a timely reminder to instructional TV producers that what may be tolerable in a classroom where the mere physical presence of a teacher makes for some kind of interaction soon becomes intolerable on a TV screen that reflects an image of an already dull reality. Finally, the junior faculty members who were called upon to provide student supportive instruction — follow-up discussions — often had negative things to say about the medium as well.

At the present time, now that the factors that encouraged the use of closed-circuit television in the first place — severe overcrowding, faculty shortages — are no longer major problems, interest has declined. Medical, dental, and other professional schools still find CCTV systems useful to transmit clinical, surgical, and other procedures to locations outside the originating classroom or laboratory. Colleges and universities still find it a valuable adjunct. Some make imaginative uses of it, feeding, for example, closed-circuit programs into cable TV systems, whence they are transmitted to student dormitories and lounge areas to help students prepare for mid-terms and final examinations.

Television for Teacher Training

Television, as noted in the introduction, is seen all over the world as a way to train and retrain teachers. Distance teaching institutions in developing parts of the world (the Indonesian Open University, for example) consider teacher training, along with continuing professional development in other areas vital to the national economy, primary goals.

In the early days of its romance with instructional television, the Ford Foundation supported a broadcast project in Texas that banded together teacher-training colleges in the state, the state department of education, and eighteen community television stations. A student, qualified in other respects, could earn a temporary teaching certificate by completing a year's training. He or she took courses on television and enrolled in one of the participating colleges for credit. No other state, as had been anticipated by Ford officials, adopted the Texas model. Texas itself abandoned the project when outside support ceased. Recruits were too few and operational costs too high to justify continuation of the program with local funds.

The Chicago TV College, which started in 1956 with a three-year grant from the Ford Foundation, demonstrated, however, that teacher training and recruitment could be done on open broadcast television on a cost-effective basis. The major objective of the Chicago project, as we shall see shortly, was something else, and the teacher-training service came about rather through serendipity than through design. Since the TV College was an extension of a community college system, all its courses were at the lower-division undergraduate level, that is, at the freshman or sophomore level. Some teacher-training courses, however, were suitable for offering at either the lower- or upper-division levels, and the two public teachers colleges then in Chicago accepted credit for them in transfer. In fact, credit earned could be used to satisfy professional education requirements if the student already held a bachelor's degree in a subject area and was seeking a temporary teaching certificate for Illinois schools, or, if the student was already a certified teacher, he or she could fulfill in-service training requirements. Eventually, several teacher-training courses were offered jointly by the community college system and the two teachers colleges, with students earning advanced-level credit at the latter. While the teacher shortage was at its height in the 1960s, enrollments were large, with a course in educational psychology attracting over 400 students in each of three different offerings and over 500 in another.[12] The program was discontinued in the early 1970s when the need for teachers abated and the participating teachers colleges were reorganized into comprehensive universities.

Some Early Experiments

The first chronicler of college courses on television, Robert Carlisle, was himself a pioneer instructional TV producer and director. He speaks from experience when he tells us that the middle 1950s were crucial years. There were failed projects enough. Many instructors and students alike, not unlike instructors and students now, did not welcome television courses with open arms. Still, there have been enough successes to keep television as one alternative path to college study for men and women who either choose to, or have to, study and learn at a distance from the classroom and live teachers. A prime source of information about this period is the *Compendium of Televised Education,* which was published at Michigan State University every year for some years under the editorial direction of Professor Lawrence E. McKune. In 1956, this compilation reported that some 300,000 were enrolled in postsecondary level TV courses. Readers should always be aware, however, that figures like these must be taken with a grain of salt, just as telecourse enrollment figures published currently are hardly accurate. The figures at times are not adjusted to show student dropouts, and do not always distinguish between the number of course enrollments and the actual student headcount. (The same student may be enrolled in several courses.)

In assessing this early period in college-level instructional television, we must always keep in mind that colleges had not yet learned how to incorporate televised courses into their programs of study. Many offered TV courses in a desultory way, with little or no planning, lured by the novelty or the sudden possibility of reaching out electronically to thousands. This was happening at a time when there were growing demands for nontraditional learning opportunities for adults. Some of the experimenters, whose commitment usually proved to be half-hearted and short-lived, found that many television students dropped out because they felt deprived of support. Others found that, although many adults said before the courses were televised that they would watch them, very few troubled to enroll for credit.

Yet in 1956, as Carlisle reports, the extension division at Harvard University and Boston's WGBH-TV, then called an ETV station, agreed to offer TV courses cooperatively. In the same year, the Chicago TV College, funded by the Ford Foundation for the Advancement of Education for a trial three-year period, inaugurated its telecasts of college courses over WTTW-TV, Chicago's ETV station. The next year, 1957, saw the start of *Sunrise Semester* on the CBS TV network. Just a year later, another commercial TV network, NBC, presented *Continental Classroom,* which made its debut in part as a result of the furor over the deficiencies of U.S. science education made so painfully apparent by the Soviets' launching of Sputnik into outer space.

Mention should also be made of the short-lived but notable New York City Metropolitan Educational Television Association, chartered by the New York State Board of Regents to air courses and cultural programs for adults. This association was a forerunner of the associations and consortia so common currently in instructional television. One of its organizers called television an ideal way to reach "older, better, brighter, and eager" students. He was talking about the adult students who higher educators believed to be "out there" in large numbers. These are the people who prove to be successful in television media-based instruction: highly motivated, leading busy lives, eager for instruction at times and places that suit their convenience. In any event, between 1957 and 1959, META presented college courses accredited by various institutions in the New York metropolitan area, telecast at first by a commercial station and later by a noncommercial one.

Finally, any discussion of significant early efforts at presenting college-level courses on television should include the State University of New York's University of the Air, which operated from 1966 until 1971. The failure of this laudable project represents one of the saddest chapters in the history of nontraditional teaching. Its failure stemmed from factors beyond the control of its directors. For one thing, the University of the Air boasted only a small repertory of televised courses. As other projects have discovered, frequent repetition of the same courses leads to declining enrollments. Off-campus credit audiences for TV courses are not like student bodies for conventional courses, with a sizable class of freshmen just out of high school waiting to take the place of last year's class. Rather, it is helpful to liken the audience for TV courses to a well whose level must be allowed to recover once it has been lowered. Unfortunately for the University of the Air, there were few suppliers of high-quality TV courses at the time.

The other factor that predestined the project to failure had to do with control of the broadcast and transmission facilities required. Even though the University of the Air had formed a statewide network of the state's public TV stations, it exercised no control over the transmitters used to broadcast the courses. The licenses for them were held by local community groups. Thus, the University of the Air was at the mercy of local public TV station managers whenever they tried to negotiate air time for their courses. They found themselves at an even further disadvantage when their small library of courses became redundant and station managers rightfully complained about the redundancy.

INFLUENCE OF THE OPEN LEARNING MOVEMENT

In the introduction, the reader's attention was called to a comment made by Walter Perry, the first vice rector of the media-based British Open University. He commented on the coming together of a worldwide demand by adults for educational opportunities and the happy appearance of the means to satisfy this demand at a reasonable cost: the mass media, especially radio and television.

As higher educators in the United States know, the demand Perry spoke of was also heard in this country. In retrospect, however, it seems that in part the clamor may have been more illusory than real, more induced than genuine. The strong demand was being felt outside the United States, in regions where postsecondary education was designed only for the young and the privileged, or where, as in the underdeveloped nations, higher education hardly existed for any significant portion of the population. In the United States, however, one suspects that the demand, though present to a degree, was largely a projection of assumptions of adult educators and media specialists who were catching the ears of officials of funding agencies. Much of the enthusiasm in this country was inspired by the success of the BOU. In addition, demographic factors supplied further impetus. An aging population suggested a stronger demand for leisure-time adult education. Likewise, there always is a desire in adults for vocational/occupational change and improvement, and in this so-called postindustrial period, when occupational skills are becoming obsolete and new ones are needed, there is even greater demand. Yet as the experience of certain projects made clear, there was no groundswell for the establishment of full-scale nontraditional or open colleges and universities like the BOU. After all, public and private colleges and universities are far from being in short supply in most sections of the country. A good number of them, the public community colleges in particular, have open admissions policies, and welcome students of all ages and backgrounds.

By the late 1960s and early 1970s, a number of states had commissioned individuals and organizations to draw up plans for "open" and nontraditional universities that would enable adults to earn college degrees in unconventional ways. Existing conventional colleges and universities established or revived external degree and nontraditional degree programs.[13] Some expressly nontraditional institutions were created. A good example is the State University of New York's Empire State College, which appeared in 1971, and which permits its students to earn credit for relevant "real-life" experiences and independent study of all kinds. Empire State, like other such institutions, serves as a sort of collegiate broker, allowing students to combine credit earned in a variety of ways (at other institutions, through life experience, through exemption tests) into sequences that lead to degrees. Another nontraditional institution, the State University of Nebraska, which eventually expanded into an interinstitutional University of Mid-America (UMA), strongly supported by the National Institute of Education, planned its program on a strong media base, including television, radio, and the computer.

A spate of influential reports and studies, in particular several commissioned by the Carnegie Foundation, appeared to fuel the movement and place it within the formal context of American higher education.[14] Interest in some colleges, it should be noted, was aroused because of dire predictions in the mid-1970s of reduced on-campus enrollments as a result of a falling birth rate. Coupled with the anticipated decline in births were predictions of increasing longevity. The fact is that some colleges — smaller liberal arts colleges, for example — have found in this growing older population a valuable source of students, as is evidenced by the number of weekend colleges and nonconventional study plans to be found around the country.

As this book is intended to show, some colleges willing to reach out to new and previously unserved students wanted to do so in innovative ways, to take advantage of the "fortuitous convergence" of education needs and technological means Walter Perry spoke about in connection with the BOU. Funding agencies also were willing to exploit this convergence both to extend and improve instruction. Throughout the 1950s and later, the Ford Foundation had funded instructional TV projects at all educational levels with a lavish hand, spending $100 million or more. The Foundation did this because its officials believed the medium would extend and share good teaching. The federal government, through its various agencies, invested an equal amount or more. It is noteworthy that all this started at a time when, as one respected educator put it, television was regarded as the "most controversial of innovations," threatening, in the view of some teachers, to lead to "automated education, mechanized teaching, and robotized students."[15]

Ford Foundation support for instructional television was given at all levels, beginning with a grant to Montclair College in New Jersey to telecast fifth-grade history lessons to nearby schools. Support was later broadened to include in-school television instruction in Washington County, Maryland, on a county-wide basis. In higher education, it supported the already mentioned teacher-training project in Texas, as well as the TV College program in Chicago that enrolled students in the city, the surrounding county, and even in parts of northern Indiana. We have already discussed the closed-circuit TV project the Foundation helped support at Pennsylvania State University. Besides all this, the Foundation awarded major support to *Continental Classroom,* the series of college-level courses presented by NBC stations across the country. This project had as one of its purposes improving the competence of college teaching by "showcasing" outstanding teachers.

Several of the Ford projects were noteworthy successes; others were qualified successes or outright failures from which media and adult educators have learned — or ought to have learned — much of value. Judith Murphy and Ronald Gross, authors of the already cited assessment of the Ford Foundation's investment in instructional television, opened their investigation with two disarmingly blunt questions: "Has television made an impact in American schools and colleges? Has it made a worthwhile contribution to education?" Others have put the questions even more bluntly: If television were to disappear from the educational scene tomorrow, would many people miss it? When *Learning by Television* first appeared in 1966, the short answer to all the questions had to be a no, even though a reluctant one.

Yet despite failures and disappointments, television had proved itself to be an effective teaching device, the investigation concluded. In all fairness, some projects had indeed been successful, though not to the point of inspiring a host of imitators throughout the country, or to the point of threatening to displace current instructional methods.

Readers may find it instructive to look at several of the more successful of the Ford-funded instructional TV projects before moving on to one of this country's most ambitious university enterprises, to date, which was supported largely by federal grants.

Chicago's TV College

Although only modestly financed over its first three years by the Ford Foundation, Chicago's TV College became self-supporting and distinguished itself as one of this country's longest lived instructional TV projects. It still retains a vestigial existence, having been absorbed in the early 1980s by a larger innovative unit of the City Colleges of Chicago, a comprehensive community college system. TV College remained in the vanguard of television-based instructional units for almost two decades. It held this position in spite of its reliance on "talking-face" and low-budget television production. TV College was the recipient of a Ford grant to test the feasibility of offering a full two-year college program on open television. It demonstrated that this was indeed a feasible goal.

Perhaps even more importantly, TV College demonstrated to the satisfaction of an originally skeptical faculty and outside observers that college courses could be offered on television without any loss of instructional quality. Throughout its history, the project was inspected by educators from this country and abroad. It was singled out for praise by the Chicago metropolitan newspapers, a former prestigious education editor of *The New York Times,* and the authors of *Learning by*

Television themselves. A visitor from the United Kingdom once commented perceptively that it did not "go in for prestige, but for quiet, solid usefulness."[16] A crowning tribute to TV College was a visit paid it by Jennie Lee, the Minister of Culture in the labor government of Prime Minister Harold Wilson. Miss Lee was one of the prime movers of the BOU, whose planners acknowledged TV College as a "prototype."

More than 200,000 men and women enrolled in TV College. Emphasis was on serving students who watch programs in their homes, although during some few years on-campus students were permitted to watch courses in campus classrooms. More than seventy-five different courses were offered, ranging from general education courses to a variety of elective and selected occupation-oriented series.

A question always arises as to one of the conditions of the original Ford grant, that is, testing the feasibility of offering a full two-year college program on open television. Did any students actually complete the full two years? In fact, about 400 earned the Associate of Arts (A.A.) degree for study finished exclusively via television. Most of them were inmates of one of several correctional institutions whose inmates were allowed to take TV College courses. Some, however, were physically handicapped people. Sprinkled among them were a few who just preferred studying on their own.

What is of real significance to adult educators interested in those who study at a distance is that the last official report on TV Colleges, which was published in 1974, noted that some 2,200 graduates of the City Colleges of Chicago, of which TV College was an extension, had completed, on an average, a semester — or about thirty credit hours — of their work in television courses. This signaled what was to become a distinctive feature of media-based learning in this country. American nontraditional learners tend to combine the nonconventional with the conventional in achieving their goals.

As indicated above, TV College services are still available in Chicago, but now are offered under the aegis of the Chicago City-Wide College, an open college that presents a variety of nonconventional study opportunities. The Chicago Community College system now owns and operates its own UHF station, which is an affiliate of PBS. Ownership of the station allows the college to telecast courses at prime viewing hours, a luxury the original TV College never had. The Chicago City-Wide College does not produce any TV courses of its own. Instead, it airs courses of high production quality it acquires from outside sources. This is an advantage in the sense that the programs acquired have visual appeal and thus attract general viewers. It can be a disadvantage for serious off-campus viewers desirous of completing degree requirements, in that the curriculum presented on television is hit-or-miss and is often irrelevant to their needs. As we shall see later, this is a problem common to adults enrolled in off-campus, media-based programs.

What can broadcast educators learn from the Chicago TV College? For one thing, they should learn that one precondition to a lasting off-campus television education program is a sizable population base. The one afforded by the Chicago metropolitan area until the severe demographic changes of the 1970s, particularly the flight to the suburbs, was ideal. This is not to say that TV courses cannot be presented successfully and at reasonable cost in less densely populated areas, but it means that fewer courses can be offered. This, in turn, means that significant portions of degree directed programs cannot be made available to off-campus learners within a reasonable length of time.

Another valuable lesson adult educators and others can learn from the TV College story is that a schedule of television courses can be adapted to the needs of a varied audience. For example, courses can be so supported and enhanced that they can satisfy the needs of a number of groups simultaneously: gifted high school students, selected students confined to correctional institutions, occupational and professional groups, degree-seeking students, groups with special interests like the parents of young children. The TV College, too, demonstrated that, with proper instructional support, just about any course can be presented effectively on television, although some subjects, for example, the social sciences and the humanities, lend themselves more readily than others.

Some important investigations of student performance, characteristics, retention, and withdrawal patterns were conducted by TV College researchers. These findings, as we shall see later, have been confirmed and reconfirmed by later investigators.

Enrollments began to decline in the 1970s for a number of reasons, of which some were beyond the control of the project. For one thing, the Chicago area was undergoing profound demographic changes, as were other urban centers in the United States. One result was a movement of many of the people best suited for independent study from the city to the suburbs. Coupled with this was the growth of the Illinois public community college system, which resulted in two-year comprehensive colleges in all regions of the state. Before campuses had been actually constructed in their districts, provisions of the original enabling legislation allowed suburban residents to attend an existing community college in another district and charge their tuition fees back to their local common school districts. This meant, in effect, that they could take TV College courses free of charge. However, once a community college facility was in operation in their districts, they were billed for TV College enrollment at an "out-of-district" higher rate. The result was virtual elimination of out-of-city TV College registrations, which at one time had been significant. In time, the City Colleges of Chicago district itself was forced by financial necessity to impose tuition charges. Prior to the 1970s, registration had been free, with only small service fees. Even though the tuition rate imposed initially was nominal (it has risen in later years), it discouraged TV College enrollments.

The lesson to be learned from the above is obvious and is not flattering to champions of television-based instruction. At the risk of anticipating what is to come later in a section devoted to TV student characteristics, it must be pointed out here that students still do not seem to value TV courses enough to pay anything more than minimal fees for taking them. This accounts in large part for the preponderance of enrollments in telecourses offered by community colleges, since they are low-tuition institutions, whereas college and university extension fees tend to be higher. The introduction of a $5 per credit hour tuition in Chicago — that is, $15 for a typical course — resulted in a 20 percent cut in TV College enrollment. California public community colleges experienced a similar decline in TV enrollments when the state abandoned its long-standing policy of tuition-free registration. Adult educators can only hope that one day federal and state scholarship policies will regularly award tuition grants to able part-time students, including ones who enroll in television courses.

Yet, this matter can be looked at from an angle less damaging to the self-esteem of TV educators. Perhaps the amount a student is willing to pay for enrolling in a TV course is a gauge of his or her degree of motivation and seriousness, even though an employer may bear the cost. For example, engineers and technologists enrolling in a National Technological University TV course pay as much as $365 per credit hour, more than $1,000 for a 3-credit-hour course. (The National Technological University will be discussed later.)

One thing more should be noted about the Chicago TV College. Like Pennsylvania State University and others, it did for a time allow on-campus students to watch televised courses in classrooms. They viewed the same courses that were being telecast on open broadcast to adults watching in their homes. Several circumstances conspired against the venture. For one thing, classroom viewing facilities were inadequate. For another, studies of student performance showed beyond any doubt that unselected community college students must have regular follow-up instruction from live instructors if they are to have any chance of matching the performance of adult counterparts studying at home. Given their relatively low level of motivation as compared with that of adults viewing at home, these same students also showed much less tolerance for "talking-head" television.

Continental Classroom

The brief episode in the history of college-level instructional television in which *Continental Classroom* figures is a fascinating one. It is also a saddening one in that a project with so much promise was so suddenly aborted. The enterprise, which also received Ford Foundation support, was conducted in cooperation with 150 National Broadcasting Company affiliates across the nation.

The story of *Continental Classroom,* which survived from 1958 until 1963, proved once again how a number of factors can suddenly come together and become a springboard for an imaginative venture. Carlisle, in his already cited report, recounts in some detail the history of the project. His account is based in part on interviews with some of the principals of the project.[17] When the Soviets launched their Sputnik into outer space on October 4, 1957, our self-esteem as a nation was shattered. A near-orgy of self-recrimination broke out about the inadequacies of our schools in teaching science and mathematics. Our pride had been wounded by the Soviets' achievement in being the first to penetrate outer space.

All this furor sparked an idea in the head of the NBC director of public relations and education at the time, Edward Stanley. He noted that the State of New York Commissioner of Education was projecting an expenditure of some $600,000 for a special in-service course for the state's science teachers. Stanley was sure that he and his colleagues in public affairs at NBC could produce a television course that would reach the nation's science teachers for not much more. When approached, the Ford Foundation agreed to contribute a half-million dollars for the first year of the project. A number of U.S. companies also made grants to the venture. Stanley remarked in the course of a conversation with the eminent scientist James Killian, the then scientific advisor to President Eisenhower, that the resulting series would be a "continental classroom."

The first course to be telecast was *Atomic Age Physics,* designed as a refresher and an update for teachers who had studied their science before physics had been revolutionized by atomic theory. The teacher in charge of the course was Professor Harvey White of the University of California, Berkeley. In Carlisle's words, "He lined up a veritable Who's Who of American Scientists as guest lecturers."

During its brief life span, *Continental Classroom* produced courses in chemistry, mathematics, and political science. Several hundred colleges and universities throughout the country accepted credit enrollments, although their policies in awarding credit for the same course varied widely, with some granting no formal credit and others granting from two to seven credit hours. (To some extent, these variations still plague producers and distributors of college-credit courses.)

During the fourth year, the Ford Foundation decided to terminate its support. The project was thereby doomed. Some of the corporate donors hung on, however, to allow for the broadcast of one final course in U.S. Government. Ironically, this offering drew an estimated audience of about 1.5 million viewers, who, it should be noted, watched the programs at 6:30 a.m. No one course, however, ever enrolled 5,000 credit students nationwide, with 4,905 reported for the post-Sputnik *Atomic Age Physics,* broadcast between 6:00 and 6:30 a.m.

In any event, NBC concluded that the size of the audiences did not warrant the expense of their continuing the series on their own. When judged by the numbers enrolling in equivalent courses on college campuses, figures like a total viewing audience of 1 million ("auditors" in academic terms), including almost 5,000 credit enrollees in a single course, seem almost immense. The budget for the series ranged from $1.2 million to $1.5 million each year, which seems minuscule when viewed from the standpoint of commercial production costs.

What was interesting to college instructional TV producers was NBC's attitude toward the teachers involved during the life of the project. Teachers hosting a series on camera were regarded as "talent," and were paid what were handsome annual salaries for academics in those years — some $40,000. In return for such payment, the teachers surrendered any rights in reruns of programs. There were additional perquisites for them, however. For example, the network absorbed any extra costs teachers incurred in moving to the New York City area. Those presenting science courses in which demonstrations were required were provided assistants to help with laboratory set-ups, and so forth. All this was taking place while lively discussions about compensation for TV teaching and teachers' residual rights in TV courses replayed in recording were going on in professional organizations. In some parts of the country, in the New York City area in particular, teachers felt that they should, indeed, be treated as television "talent," rather than as academics employing a studio as an extension of the classroom. Status as talent would have entailed some guarantees of residual rights and control over their product, and would also have necessitated affiliation with the television performers' union.

The *Continental Classroom* professors had to work hard, but one of the producers interviewed by Carlisle stated that there were no attempts made to introduce "show biz" into programs. Professor Harvey White's studio set was a duplicate of his lecture hall at Berkeley. This information makes an interesting contribution to the debate that continues among instructional TV producers and designers as to how big a part "show biz" techniques should play in instructional programs. But before concluding that a classroom setting and performance are satisfactory for both viewers seeking informal instruction and those seeking college credit, we should remind ourselves that both the general audience and the credit students following *Atomic Age Physics* must have been motivated by a strong interest in the subject matter, and were hardly typical of unselected lower-division undergraduate audiences.

Continental Classroom stands as a noble experiment in nationalizing television courses and improving the professional status of professors who teach on television. It also proved, once and for all, something that really needed no proving, that is, the ability of an enthusiastic, personable professorial "talking face" to command and hold the attention of a large audience interested in learning. It also confirmed what has sadly been reconfirmed throughout the history of instructional television, that is, that nationally and regionally based projects seldom become fully self-supporting. Once outside subsidies disappear, the projects wither away and die.

At present, TV courses being designed and produced by several community college producers, a few state public TV authorities like the Maryland Center for Public Broadcast or the South Carolina Educational Television Authority, and, of course, the Annenberg/Corporation for Public Broadcasting Project, are the successors of the *Continental Classroom* national courses. They are produced for national markets and are employed by institutions all over the country. They are aimed not only at narrow college-credit seeking audiences but also at intellectually curious general audiences. For this reason, PBS station managers, who would have no time on their evening schedules for the more direct instructional approach of the *Continental Classroom* programs, will often play them during early evening viewing hours.

Sunrise Semester

This attempt to use the facilities of a commercial network deserves mention. The CBS network's *Sunrise Semester* led a hand-to-mouth existence from 1957 until the mid-1980s, a long run indeed for a U.S. instructional TV series. Until 1963, it was telecast locally in the New York City area, after which time it went on the network.

Its success began with a course in comparative literature presented by a telegenic professor from New York University at 6:30 a.m. Watching the programs became, in a way, a matter of New York chic. The audience was respectable, including 150 viewers who enrolled for college credit and paid the fee assessed by New York University. Local bookstores that stocked the texts discussed on television, from Stendhal to Hemingway, reported that supplies were quickly depleted.

Sunrise Semester received only modest and fitful support from its funding agencies. New York University assumed responsibility for scheduling the courses and designing the content of the programs, until the final years of the project when Bergen Community College in New Jersey took over the programming. Official enrollments were usually small, at times under twenty. Tuition charges for credit students ran as high as $250, which, of course inhibited credit enrollment. Broadcast times, from 6:00 until 6:30 a.m., discouraged all but the most determined. Yet New York University officials estimated that as many as 1 million viewers watched programs of courses while they were on the national network. Recordings of programs were not rerun because of the lack of funds to pay teachers for reuses as required by their union contracts. New York University, while it was coordinating the project, never made programs available on videocassettes for the same reason.

Despite the handicaps under which it labored, *Sunrise Semester* was remarkably long-lived. Surely it is regrettable that at least out of a sense of public responsibility, commercial broadcasters nowadays can neither provide support nor provide air time for national courses, even if they are aired at six o'clock in the morning.

The Maryland College of the Air

One other project deserves mention in a section dedicated to those who pioneered distributing instructional television courses on a regional or a national basis. The Maryland College of the Air, a state-supported public television agency, still survives and flourishes. It is worth consideration for several reasons. For one thing, the College of the Air provides a regular schedule of credit television courses for the community colleges and higher education institutions in its area that want to make them part of their extension activities. For another, within the last fifteen years, the Maryland Center for Public Broadcasting, of which it is one service, has produced high-quality TV programs, on its own or in collaboration with others, which have been adopted for use by colleges all over the country.

At the end of the 1960s, officials of the Maryland Center, prominent among them Richard Smith, Director of Development, began planning what in a few years was to become the College of the Air. Smith, who later presided over the community college consortium that determined the College of the Air's annual schedule of courses, made his own preliminary assessment of the needs of Maryland audiences, of the state of televised education at the time, and of the attitudes of the higher education community toward television for instruction. After carefully looking at the Chicago TV College record, he became convinced that the courses best suited for presentation on television were the very ones that attracted large enrollments on campus. Since these courses satisfied requirements that adult students who studied off campus wanted to complete, the courses need not have been stylish, expensive productions. What was essential was that they were instructionally sound. Therefore, he leased such courses wherever they were available, even though they might have been deficient in production finish. Courses that were not available the Maryland Center itself produced at modest cost.

Smith felt that the College of the Air should be governed by a loose association, or consortium, of community colleges using the television courses. The user colleges themselves decided what the on-the-air curriculum should be, subject, of course, to the availability of materials and the production capabilities of the Maryland Center. Member colleges were free to adopt or not to adopt any course or courses offered on the air. Whenever the Maryland Center produced a course for common use of the College of the Air, it hired whatever teachers were involved in planning and preparation upon recommendation of the consortium. The College of the Air never felt that it had, or would have, a market for an entire two-year college program on television. Smith and his associates were aware that the experience of their program would reflect that of the Chicago TV College, and that Maryland adults, like Chicago-area adults, would take advantage of television to earn credits that they would later transfer to conventional community college or four-year college programs.

In recent years, the Maryland Center has designed and produced TV courses at costs that allow it to exploit the properties of the medium. This kind of design, which makes use of professional actors as hosts and is enriched by on-location filming, film inserts, guest expertise, and so on, is more in keeping with the practice of leading TV course designers nowadays, as we shall be pointing out later on.

THE EARLY DAYS IN RETROSPECT

Other institutions and agencies could certainly have been singled out for mention among the precursors and pioneers. The ones discussed, however, are representative of college-level instructional TV development until the mid- and late-1960s. Our discussion has made it clear that the early days of college and university TV uses were not "early" in a chronological sense. Rather, they were early in the sense that practitioners were not as yet attempting to tap the distinctive presentational properties of the medium, especially as these properties are employed to capture the attention of general viewing audiences. The better programs were not so much TV programs as they were simulated and enhanced classroom lectures, and always under the control of a visible professor. If the professor was articulate, warm, and at ease in the studio, so much the better for viewers.

Producing without frills was not so much a matter of choice as it was of bitter necessity. The institutions producing the materials lacked the financial and professional resources needed for sophisticated TV production. Even in relatively well-funded projects, the prime objective was to extend classroom instruction, not to present it in a different guise. If instruction were to be improved, it would come through superior instructors, whose methods, it was hoped, would be emulated. In short, in supporting TV projects, the Ford Foundation was not primarily concerned with improving teaching by adapting the distinctive presentational properties of the medium to the instructional process, but was interested, first and foremost, in displaying effective classroom teaching to wider audiences.

As indicated earlier, the major goal of Chicago's TV College was to test the feasibility of offering a full two-year college program on open broadcast. This goal was the controlling factor in the conduct of the project for much of its life. Courses had to be produced in quantity and quickly to insure a steady flow of the materials needed to offer a full two-year program home-viewing students could complete within a reasonable time. Indeed, it was possible for a diligent student to earn the Associate of Arts degree in three years, provided he or she enrolled in TV College's summer terms.

Nonetheless, there was always a strong desire to employ television as a way of improving and altering the teaching process itself. During the 1960s and 1970s, programmed learning theories, teaching machines, and the introduction of the computer to the classroom as an aid to learning triggered lively activities in the emerging art of instructional design, or instructional technology, as it is sometimes called. College and university departments of education established subdepartments that began to train people in this art, which was defined as follows in a 1970 government report commissioned by a President's Commission on Instructional Technology:

> ... a systematic way of designing, carrying out, and evaluating the total process of learning and teaching in terms of specific objectives, based on research in human learning and communication, and employing a combination of human and non-human resources to bring about more effective instruction.[18]

Producers and teachers alike soon learned that TV courses, to be effective and distinctive learning experiences, must be planned as integrated systems of video, print, face-to-face activities, even mixes of other media — radio, the computer — wherever feasible. Ideally, each component should complement the other. Once the BOU was in full operation, its investigators began speculating about and sorting out the instructional chores the various components could best perform. One consequence of this was that more care was taken with selecting the textbooks and preparing the printed study guides and study aids to accompany the TV programs. Video, in consequence, was no longer being used to purvey information that students could get just as well from their textbooks and study guides. The number of video programs in a course was reduced from as many as forty-five to twenty-six in TV courses produced in the United States. The length of the individual program was standardized at roughly thirty minutes. (BOU producer–designers make video an even smaller proportion of courses, including as many programs as seem appropriate to a particular topic.)

ATTITUDES TOWARD TELEVISION TEACHING

Administrators and Faculty

At times, only the outside observer has the perspective and necessary detachment to make a realistic assessment of a project. In 1969, while the BOU was in its final planning stages, *The Times* of London sent a reporter to this country to look at several American television-based higher education projects. Among those she visited were two described in these pages, New York's University of the Air and Chicago's TV College. As already noted, Jennie Lee, the Labor Government minister responsible for the White Paper calling originally for a University of the Air in the United Kingdom, had herself spent a day at the TV College. The reporter stated in her story that, in this country, "so far" — that is, until 1969 — television had supplied some "fringe education." She went on, however, to pass on the following insight: ". . . by failure of commitment and imagination from the top America's educational needs and television's potential have barely been brought together."[19]

Her observation was not only sound at that time, but also still applies to U.S. higher education and television. In any event, it was not until the 1970s that there were signs that a substantial top-level commitment to television might emerge. Prominent educators like Alvin Eurich and Samuel Gould, both former presidents of the large State University of New York system and both influential with the educational foundations, championed television along with other nontraditional modes of teaching and learning. On the whole, however, televised education was regarded variously as a peripheral activity that brought in some odd students, as a nuisance, or as a necessary evil in some of the universities using closed-circuit television to cover large-enrollment, multisection classes. Faculty attitudes ranged from indifference to outright hostility. For the most part, only those actively involved with the medium ever became enthusiastic about its potential. Alvin Eurich summed up prevailing faculty feelings when he referred to television as a "most controversial of innovations," a statement quoted earlier.

Some teachers, no doubt, expressed genuine fear about being displaced by the TV camera, whereas others felt just as sincerely that TV courses would debase academic coinage and allow students to earn college credits on the cheap. Still others were convinced that courses on television could never be true academic or intellectual equivalents of classroom courses, if only because of the absence of direct face-to-face contact between student and teacher and the loss of classroom give-and-take. Some faculty members (and administrators) argued that courses taken off campus by television should be so designated on students' transcripts. This, in fact, is still done by some extension divisions offering TV courses, although not by most. Fortunately, however, most teachers kept open minds and were willing to be persuaded, except, perhaps, in those institutions where the bad taste of unpopular closed-circuit TV experiences lingered.

There were, of course, faculty concerns about compensation for teaching on television. After all, studio teaching imposes conditions quite different from those in the conventional classroom. Inevitably, parallels were drawn between compensation patterns in commercial television and universities. Then, too, what residual rights should teachers retain in their courses, should the course be replayed in recording? These concerns were strengthened as videotape players and recorders became less expensive. Teacher organizations vied with each other in preparing policy statements on uses of television in education. As early as 1962, the American Association of University Professors approved a detailed policy on uses of television in colleges and universities, the gist of which was that faculty must retain control and have final say on how the medium is to be employed.

As teaching on television became more common, not surprisingly, there was continuous and often rancorous discussion in faculty senates and councils as to how teachers should be paid for it and what rights they were to have in the fruits of their labors in case of reuses and adoptions by other institutions. Concern was expressed, too, about how teachers could protect their scholarly reputations in the event recorded courses should become outdated and changes in content should be needed.

Issues of compensation for TV teachers proved especially complicated, since they involved those who present the courses on camera as well as instructors on campus who supply the follow-up and supplemental instruction for students enrolled in TV courses. The questions were attacked in various ways by various institutions. Colleges with faculty covered by collective bargaining agreements — community colleges, for the most part — often have provisions in their union contracts governing the conditions under which nontraditional teaching functions are to be carried out. Teachers presenting courses on camera are often released from their normal duties, and are paid an additional sum over and above what they normally receive. The length of release from their usual duties depends on how elaborate the production is to be and how much time must be devoted to content preparation. For a well-designed course that is to be made available for use nationally, a full calendar year's release is not unusual. In cases where studio production is modest or minimal and the course consists of essentially a lecturing professor, the presenter may be awarded an extra assignment and additional compensation over and above his or her normal teaching assignment on campus. There are understandings as to compensation in the event of reruns of courses and uses by other institutions. Usually, when teachers involved in preparing and presenting TV courses that are to be marketed nationally are awarded extra compensation, there is an understanding that this stipend precludes the payment of any residual fees.

Likewise, support instructors are recruited and compensated for their work in a variety of ways. Some colleges employ part-time instructors or qualified graduate assistants specifically for providing TV supportive instruction. Others employ full-time members of their faculties, awarding them partial release from regular teaching duties or paying them additional stipends. All payment for support instructors is posited on the recognition that this kind of instruction involves less preparation and fewer responsibilities than conventional teaching. Some colleges compensate support teachers in accordance with often complicated, even bizarre, formulas that take into account the number of students they are responsible for and the nature of their duties in a given course — that is, are there papers to be actually read and graded, or are the exercises objective ones that can be machine-graded, and so on? Needless to say, the role of the support instructor has yet to be clearly defined, and, as a result, there are no standard patterns of remuneration. Unfortunately, except in some community colleges where sizable numbers of faculty members are actively involved in support instruction, the position of the support instructor has remained in a professional no man's land. Another factor clouding the status of support instructors is that many successful TV students never avail themselves of their services as counselors or tutors, but see them only as record-keepers.

Much of the faculty concern about televised instruction, even though it still surfaces on occasion, proved to be a tempest in a teapot. Colleges and universities making regular use of television soon arrived at formal or informal understandings about its uses, compensation patterns, replay policies, and so forth with their faculties. Faculty fears about television replacing teachers and reducing costs of education soon were dispelled when teachers were not replaced by the tube and the costs of presenting TV courses were not low. A long-running and successful project like Chicago's TV College considered itself cost-effective if its costs were no higher than those of instructional costs in the conventional classroom.

Unfortunately, however, for proponents of TV uses in continuing education and extension, TV instruction was established outside the mainstream higher education interests. Some faculty members, too, though not always acting out of disinterested motives, continued to express alarm that TV courses for which academic credit is awarded by some institutions are less than academically reputable. Their point was sometimes well taken in that some community colleges did offer full credit courses that fell into the gray area between formal instruction and informal leisure-time adult education — courses in sketching, home decorating, mid-life career change. However, such offerings are no longer bones of contention, since most state authorities in these days of fiscal austerity no longer will fund community colleges for informal adult and leisure-time courses. We should note at this point, however, that, whenever TV courses have been assessed by academic committees, they have been deemed as demanding as equivalent courses offered on campus. As recently as several years ago, some faculty members in California again raised questions as to the content of several courses presented by public community colleges. The review committee appointed by the state universities system found the courses to be academically sound. We should also remember that some courses offered on campuses for regular academic credit fall into the gray area mentioned above.

Students

Much more will be said later about students who take TV courses when we look at what the research tells us about student attitudes toward instructional television. In the early years, which are our concern at the moment, there was much student dissatisfaction with the use of television for classroom instruction, as the references to the Ford Foundation–supported assessments attest. At the college level, part of the unfavorable attitude stemmed from a lack of adequate support for students enrolled in TV courses. Students complained that they were not given opportunity enough to meet with tutors or support instructors, or were not provided study materials that allowed them to gauge their progress in the course. As with traditional correspondence study, dropout, or attrition, was high. At the other extreme, some early TV projects enrolling adult students off campus made unreasonable demands on students, requiring frequent, even weekly, attendance at on-campus seminars or class meetings, forgetting that adults take courses on television because of constraints on their time.

Students enrolled in closed-circuit television on campuses were also disenchanted on more general grounds. Some felt that they were being short-changed or relegated to second-rate status. Others felt, as Murphy and Gross reported in *Learning by Television,* that they were being denied any genuine personal contact. Many complained of the boredom of TV lectures, with the faces on camera too often droning on and on in poorly lighted sets.

The important thing is that educators and instructional TV producers learned much from these discouragingly unfavorable attitudes. We shall be considering some of what they learned in later chapters.

Finding Its Place in Higher Education

A COMING TOGETHER OF FACTORS

Reference has already been made to Walter Perry's comment about several factors converging to help make the United Kingdom's Open University the most significant attempt yet to harness the presentational and distributional powers of television for higher education. The same factors came together in the United States to make television more than a novelty and gimmick in higher education. Still another factor was at work on this side of the Atlantic: the immediate and spectacular success of the BOU itself.

Perry named the insistent demand for educational opportunities in postwar Europe an important precondition for the BOU's success. It has also been noted that the same demand was heard in this country, although to a markedly lesser degree. In the late 1960s and early 1970s, some prominent American educators were fervently advocating "open learning," external degree programs, and lifelong learning. The labels varied, but the idea was the same, not that external degrees, or degrees earned for study completed at places often remote from campuses, were new ideas. London University, to cite only one famous example, had been offering external degree programs since the last century.

There was strong feeling that too many Americans had been deprived of higher education through no fault of their own. Others who had had a chance had not profited by it for reasons other than intellectual incapacities. Many had been immature, unmotivated, or not yet ready.

Does not anyone who sincerely wants it and is determined to make the most of it deserve a second chance?

It is difficult to pronounce with any certainty how many adult Americans really feel educationally deprived. Yet, as newspaper and magazine readers know, respondents to questionnaires regularly say that they feel their growth as adults has been stunted and their path to social and financial advancement has been blocked by the lack of opportunity to acquire higher education. Unfortunately, as planners of open learning projects have discovered to their dismay, only a small proportion of those who express the need ever take advantage of open learning opportunities when these opportunities are made available to them. Still people in the United States, even more so than people in other industrialized societies, are credentials-obsessed. A high school diploma is necessary for even the most unskilled occupation. Their lack of college degrees makes promotion to managerial or supervisory status unlikely for many worthy men and women. Yet, while conceding all this, we must still bear in mind that, in most sections of this country, there is no shortage of institutions — vocational centers, high school adult education programs, community colleges, college and university extension divisions — that offer working adults study opportunities during late afternoon and evening hours, on Saturdays and even over weekends. Some of the programs, especially those offered by public vocational training centers and community colleges, entail only nominal or modest costs for the student.

Nonetheless, some ambitious adults find it impossible to enroll in even a single course in a conventional institution. Attending classes over a period long enough to enable some adults to earn degrees or certificates is an impossible and cruel dream. Researchers querying adults who enroll in open and off-campus learning programs to determine what the obstacles are that prevent their studying in conventional ways are not surprised by the recurrent answers. Distance from the institution, lack of time for travel and regular attendance, age, fatigue, and inconvenience are the most common answers.[1] Both younger and older adults enroll in TV courses because they best enable them to overcome obstacles of time and inconvenience. The competing demands on their time and energies made by work and family responsibilities preclude their traveling back and forth to attend classes regularly.

Many Americans were, and are, denied education beyond high school by turns of fortune's wheel — poverty, underprivilege, racial and ethnic disadvantage. One answer to this, short of eradicating poverty and injustice, is to devise new paths to educational credentialing through the mass media that reach virtually everyone in our society. The following statement from the opening page of the 1973 *Catalogue of the State University of New York* describing proficiency examinations that satisfy some requirements for the New York Regents external degree, an open or nontraditional study mode, deserves quotation if only because it expresses the outlook of educators concerned with equalizing educational opportunities:

> In a society which increasingly demands academic credentials as proof of competency ... methods must be developed to acknowledge the accomplishments of those who have acquired college level knowledge and skills by means other than traditional classroom study.

This statement, commendable in its offer of hope to those excluded from the conventional academic credentialing systems, discloses a premise that underlies the thinking of many who plan and administer open colleges and universities in this country. This premise is that there should be unquestioning acceptance of a credit-hour system that lays as much stress on the process by which college credit is earned, for example, the number of hours spent sitting in classrooms, as on the outcomes, which are demonstrated by knowledge or skills. In the early days of instructional television, producers and designers had to take great pains to satisfy traditionalists on campus that the TV lessons, which are only one single element of a total video course, approximated in number and length the number of class sessions in a conventional course.

The proficiency examinations mentioned above, it happens, were one of the means introduced in the 1970s to permit mature students to demonstrate knowledge they had gained through their reading or work and life experiences. The College Level Exemption (CLEP) testing program was developed to allow students to exempt themselves from certain course requirements and even earn credit for the subjects in which they showed proficiency, depending, of course, on the policies of the institution in which they were enrolling. Such tests, however, did little to advance the cause of egalitarianism in higher education, since relatively few adults have done enough reading in the social sciences or physical sciences, or have the work or life experiences to equip them to pass college-level proficiency examinations.

In short, American open learning agencies are usually cast as adjuncts to, or as interinstitutional extensions of, existing institutions. Only the two-year community colleges, whose charters commit them to serving all segments of their communities, seemed willing to bring a range of nontraditional practices, including media-based instruction, into the mainstream of their activities. It is saddening, therefore, to look back at the important role projected for open learning and open institutions when the dream was fresh. The published proceedings of the First Annual National Conference on Open Learning in Higher Education, held in 1973 and sponsored by the University of Nebraska and the Great Plains National Instructional Television Library, strike even a noncynical reader twenty-five years and more later as almost touchingly innocent. One of the featured speakers, the then president of the University of Nebraska, described the newly established State University of Nebraska (the open university that later with federal support was to evolve into the media-based UMA). His presentation was entitled "The Future Begins Today." Another speaker conjured up a vision of "millions of people, adults of all ages and circumstances who are eager for and even demanding opportunities to learn more about something."[2] In all fairness to the latter speaker, an astute administrator and educator, it must be added that he did see "difficulties and obstacles" interfering with the growth of open learning.

At about this very time, it should be noted, a stream of reports commissioned by prestigious foundations and federal agencies, and authored by distinguished educators, were advocating a higher education designed for students who needed educational options at all stages of their lives.[3] Such sanguine projections, of course, were prompted to a large degree by the success of the BOU in the United Kingdom.

THE BRITISH OPEN UNIVERSITY (BOU):
THE PIPE DREAM COME TRUE

This book, as stated at the outset, is limited to reviewing and assessing uses of television in American higher education. However, it must be clear to the reader by now that the BOU cannot be passed over without some notice, since its success had such great impact on media and nonmedia-based projects alike in both this country and around the world. In fact, there were attempts, some supported by private foundation funding, to import and "naturalize" BOU teaching materials for use in this country. One distinguished American adult educator contended that the year of the chartering of the BOU, 1969, was as important a date in the history of higher education as 1860, the year the U.S. land grant colleges were established: "Each provided a serious sustained learning opportunity for large numbers of people for whom higher education had never been available."[4] In any event, by the early 1980s, the BOU had become the United Kingdom's largest degree-granting institution, claiming some 80,000 students. When initial plans for the institution were being discussed in 1966, the influential *Times Educational Supplement,* voicing the general opinion in the British higher education establishment, had derided the BOU as a "pipe dream."

This is not the place to go into a detailed account of the origin and record of the BOU. Walter Perry, the long-time BOU vice chancellor, or chief administrative officer, has written a readable history replete with interesting personal anecdotes about the foreseen and unforeseen perils that arose in the course of planning and actual foundation. The very notion originated as a political ploy to enliven the languishing political campaign of Labor Prime Minister Harold Wilson. The idea was first advanced in a 1963 Glasgow speech, and ultimately refined and presented in a 1966 landmark government White Paper. It was proposed originally as a "University of the Air." Perry reports that Prime Minister Wilson was resolved to turn "technological advances in the media of mass communications to the service of education."[5]

In 1965, Wilson had asked Jennie Lee, a subminister of arts in his government, to take on the responsibility for the proposed institution. Among other things, she insisted in the White Paper just cited that a TV channel be reserved for the venture. More importantly, she promised that students would not be offered "a makeshift project inferior in quality to other universities." The name University of the Air was eventually dropped in 1966 in favor of Open University, better to suggest the goal of opening higher education to all. The change of name proved a happy one for another reason. A relatively small proportion of BOU instruction is carried by television, with print carrying the main load and other media — radio, audiocassettes, the computer — playing important parts.

The key to the BOU's success lies in its charter as a freestanding university, empowered to grant general and first-class degrees. In addition, its part-time students can earn degrees in what is a reasonable period of time, in some cases as quickly as within three years.

Another important factor in the appeal of the BOU lies in its articulated curricular sequences. The curriculum is based on a Scottish university model (Jennie Lee, now deceased, was a Scot, as is Walter Perry, now Lord Perry), with students completing six year-long courses for a general degree, eight for an honors degree. The course of study, a demanding one, is a mixture of rich multidisciplinary introductory and advanced-level work. Individual courses are designed by teams of academics and technologists working in close collaboration. In recent years, this team approach has been questioned by some on the grounds that it is overly expensive and time-consuming. However, Perry has remained a vigorous champion of it, insisting that it is the one element that makes the BOU curriculum distinctive and particularly rewarding.

The teaching methodology combines large measures of correspondence study, tutorial sessions at study centers located throughout the United Kingdom, yearly student attendance at two-week summer sessions on British university campuses, computerized exercises, TV programs, and radio and audiocassette programs. The frequency of TV programs varies with the subject matter of the courses. In recent years, with mounting TV production costs and increased economic austerity, sophisticated production has been cut to a minimum. As often happens in the United States as well, tensions between the professional broadcasters and the academicians are not infrequent, despite the fact that the government, which controls broadcast, has mandated BBC cooperation with BOU staff and has even constructed a production facility at BOU headquarters.

By 1968, the BOU had awarded some 39,000 degrees, a truly remarkable record. Officials insist that interest in the programs remains high, with more applicants each year than available places. In recent years, the Conservative government has imposed increasingly stringent budget constraints on all of higher education in the United Kingdom, and has demanded that the BOU begin to emphasize shorter curricular sequences that lead to occupational/professional credentialing, particularly in technical and technology areas.

Every observer raises the question as to how "open" the BOU really is. Has it drawn the working class students, traditionally deprived of higher education opportunities, in the numbers Jennie Lee originally envisioned? The institution does have an open admissions policy, the one exception being that students below age twenty-one are usually not accepted. After admitting eighteen-year-olds for a short time, officials decided to discontinue accepting them, since, on the whole, their performance showed that they lacked the maturity to study on their own. The university also, whenever warranted, advises applicants whose weak educational background may handicap them to take preparatory courses before entering the program.

As for the recurring query about working class students coming to the program, the answer so far has been disappointing. Adults from less privileged segments of the general population — women and working class representatives, in particular — have been pretty much underrepresented. (This, it should be noted, is partly similar to the U.S. experience with nontraditional learning. Blue collar workers tend to be markedly underrepresented, whereas, interestingly enough, in the U.S. women are markedly overrepresented.) Occupational groups such as teachers and technicians have also enrolled in the BOU in numbers disproportionate to their representation in the general population, comprising a large segment of the total study body. After looking at data on student characteristics, an observer comes away with a strong impression that BOU students on the whole possess the educational qualifications that would gain them admission to conventional British universities. Their success rate proves this. By the end of 1974, 54 percent of the 1971 entry group had been awarded degrees. As many as 80 percent earned course credit in the first two years of operations. (Attrition is higher at the advanced level.) American nontraditional educators teaching adults at a distance should note the BOU practice of permitting applicants to enroll on a trial basis before they pay their fees and make their registration official. This obviates some problems with the dropout rate among students not really committed or suited to independent study.[6]

There can be no question that the BOU is one of the great educational achievements of this century. Yet, it is legitimate to ask how long the steady and continuing adult demand for degree-directed study will persist to warrant the maintenance of an institution of the magnitude of the BOU. Once the backlogged demand of nondegreed teachers and technicians has been satisfied, will the numbers of adult degree seekers seriously decline? Officials insist that there is a continuing "demand for degree-directed study among working adults."[7] During its first twenty years of service, the institution filled an educational void and provided adults with educational programs other British institutions could not or would not supply. The present British government's feeling that the country has greater need for technical/occupational curricula below the degree level may, perhaps, be well founded and signal the future lines of direction for the BOU.

ATTEMPTS TO IMPORT THE BOU TO THE UNITED STATES

Some American adult educators were so bedazzled by the success of the BOU that they hurried to adapt BOU materials to uses in this country.

U.S. multi-media specialists and educational technologists wondered if the program could be reproduced in an American version. It is instructive, in this connection, to recall a comment made by a BOU representative at the Nebraska Open Learning Conference mentioned above. He warned those present about "myths" that had grown up in the United States. One was that the BOU is a university for the working class. Another is that it is a TV university. Indeed, only a very small portion of a student's time is spent watching a TV set. Instruction is largely print-based, with the student studying materials published by the BOU itself and other publishers.[8] Anyone acquainted with U.S. off-campus and remote teaching projects will agree that his timely warning went largely unheeded.

Some U.S. adult educators felt that BOU course materials, with or without their TV supporting programs, could be "naturalized," especially the multidisciplinary courses. Interest on this side of the Atlantic was so keen for several years that the BOU opened and maintained a marketing and distribution office in this country. The Carnegie Foundation even funded a project to assess the feasibility of employing the materials in this country. Several large universities, including Maryland, Houston, Southern Illinois, and Rutgers, were involved in the trial. Only the University of Maryland still uses the materials in its own extension division and through the International University Consortium of which it is a member. Employment by the other universities was short-lived.

Again, anyone familiar with U.S. higher education formats can recognize the problems that arise with adaptation of course materials designed for use in a British setting. There was never any question as to the academic quality of the courses. On the contrary, some American faculty thought some of the introductory materials, especially in mathematics, too difficult for the average American freshman or sophomore. Another formidable problem lay in the fact that the BOU multidisciplinary foundation courses run for a full year and are the equivalent of a full year, or thirty credit hours, in U.S. academic currency. American students and colleges are accustomed to discrete courses that generate three to five hours of credit, or a little more when laboratory experiences are involved.

Even though not insuperable if a user institution was willing to modify and drastically repackage the materials, the obstacles to adoption by U.S. universities were genuine ones. Accompanying video programs posed problems of a broader, cultural kind, although some of the humanities and social sciences programs were excellent enough to counteract problems posed by British accents and professorial mannerisms.

Other barriers to adoption soon surfaced. Delays and problems in ordering and acquiring required texts were encountered. Some would-be experimenters also felt that the materials were overly expensive to lease or purchase in view of the modest enrollments they could anticipate.

All in all, these brave attempts proved misbegotten. One, perhaps, has achieved a modest and lasting success, the International University Consortium (IUC), established originally in 1980 as the National University Consortium for Telecommunications in Teaching with support from the Carnegie Foundation, the Maryland Center for Public Broadcast, and the University of Maryland's University College. The name was changed when several Canadian colleges joined the consortium.

The International University Consortium (IUC)

A former director of IUC's forerunner, The National University Consortium, accounted for what he considered the success of the consortium as follows: "[It is] a model that builds on the strengths of the present structures of American higher education."[9] That is, each of the consortium's members awards whatever academic credit it thinks proper for the courses offered by IUC, charges its own fees, and is actively involved in the governance of the consortium. Some of the courses, as indicated, were adapted from the BOU curriculum. Others, however, are developed in this country at the Maryland Center for Public Broadcast. In fact, IUC at present has effectively abandoned any reliance it had on BOU learning materials and is becoming much like other U.S. telecommunications consortia, either producing (through the Maryland Center) or acquiring courses for the use of its members elsewhere.

One of IUC's original objectives, it should be noted, was to acquire, produce, or otherwise provide enough course materials over the six-year period beginning in 1980 to allow member colleges to award Bachelor of Arts degrees to students completing the program. The inducement to join IUC lay in its providing a member college academically sound curricula that the user can revise to suit its particular needs, adopt totally, or merge with already existing off-campus programs.

The financial base of IUC is like that of many off-campus teaching associations. Members pay yearly membership fees and are assessed a fee for each officially enrolled student. Part of the fees is shared with stations that broadcast TV programs and with the BOU if their materials are employed. The hope of consortium officials is that, once enrollments are high enough, operations will become self-supporting. Unfortunately, credit enrollments in such consortially based projects tend to be small, and, as a consequence, the projects tend to lead a precarious existence.

THE UNIVERSITY OF MID-AMERICA (UMA)

The most ambitious project attempting to create a native equivalent of the BOU was the University of Mid-America (UMA), which began in 1974 and lasted until 1982 when the National Institute for Education (NIE), a now discontinued unit of the U.S. Department of Education, terminated its funding. UMA, a regional consortium, grew out of the already mentioned State University of Nebraska, a venture that combined the resources of Nebraska Educational Television, one of this country's exemplary state-controlled educational networks, and the University of Nebraska. Officials hoped that UMA eventually could be expanded into a nationally based open institution, or American Open University.[10] When its board of trustees dissolved UMA, they also abandoned planning for an American Open University, which agency was eventually absorbed by the New York Institute of Technology and offers self-paced courses to distant learners via personal computer.

For those interested in the history of multi-media-based higher education UMA stands as an imaginative concept and an instructive failure. Presumably, the Department of Education must have seen in the plan as submitted for funding a potential model of a media-based distance teaching institution, for it provided generous financial support over seven or eight years. Of course, strong federal support of projects is not necessarily a sign that the funding agency regards the project as a model. Sometimes it is an indication that the project had aggressive support by a congressional delegation.

UMA planning appears to have been carried out carefully on the basis of a determination of adult student needs for off-campus instruction. In fact, the American Open University projected as a culminating activity was to be a response to what was disclosed by the U.S. Census of 1980, that is, that about 18 million Americans had earned college credit but never went on to complete degrees. The assumption, hardly justifiable in view of what we have learned, was that several million Americans would jump at the chance to finish degrees in an institution that did not require conventional class attendance and other traditional trappings. After transferring whatever credit they had earned to the innovative institution, they could earn additional credit through proficiency examinations and relevant work and life experience. They could also earn credit in multi-media courses to be completed in their homes.

UMA, a consortium of eleven midwestern universities, undertook four kinds of activities during its brief, but exciting and well-publicized, span of years: (1) designing and producing multi-media courses for adults studying off campus; (2) sponsoring and conducting research on adult and distance learning; (3) guiding and assisting its member universities in supporting their students studying at a distance; (4) marketing its teaching materials, that is, the media-based courses and accompanying materials, throughout the country.

The project's initial commitment to the production of high-quality multi-media products, TV courses in particular, was a heavy one financially, much heavier, indeed, than adult students, if they had been polled, would have judged necessary or desirable. Some students found the flashy "show-biz" elements in early TV programs distracting, even silly, rather than helpful to learning. In later productions, UMA began to rely on fewer TV courses and on fewer video programs per course.

Course designers adopted the BOU team approach, joining together content specialists from the faculties of consortium members, instructional technologists and designers, TV staff, and evaluation experts. Some version of this approach, as we shall see, despite its cumbersomeness, is pretty much the standard for the U.S. instructional TV producers and designers who market their products nationally, as indeed UMA did.

In all candor, one cannot regard UMA's record in serving students as ever being particularly impressive. Between 1973 and 1982, UMA had some 15,000 credit enrollments in its eleven consortium members. Looked at in the proper context, this figure is significant. After all, the project was centered in a part of the country that is not densely populated. U.S. experience with students studying at a distance via television indicates that, as a rule of thumb, no more than about 2 percent of the general population have a strong enough interest in higher education opportunities actually to enroll in TV courses. UMA, however, employed a variety of media to deliver its instruction, including in addition to broadcast and cable television, FM radio, audiotapes, telephone, and even the newspaper.

Naturally, it would be unfair, even churlish, to dismiss UMA out of hand as a failure.[11] For one thing, it resulted in some helpful investigations of adult and distance learning. For another, as just suggested, it dispelled illusory notions as to the potential size of enrollments in nontraditionally presented college-credit courses. All this has taught others — or should have taught them — that a sustainable nontraditional learning program, particularly a media-based one, must be in a reasonably well populated area, unless, as some community college users of TV courses are now doing, it can draw each term on a population of students who are enrolled concurrently in classes taught conventionally on campus.

UMA's failure to survive or make any lasting impact is attributable to more than any single cause. One big cause was curriculum policy. Its courses seemed to be selected at random, the selection ungoverned by any discernible rationale relating to student needs or goals. The consequence was that a serious, well-motivated adult was not given a chance to complete via media-based study any significant portion of a curriculum, credit for which he or she could later transfer to a conventional institution. (By the way, had the opportunity to transfer been available to a student, there was always the possibility that one or more of the UMA consortium institutions would not have honored the credit, since each member reserved the right to accredit or not accredit UMA courses.) The lack of curriculum rationale undoubtedly resulted from the early commitment to high-quality TV production. The costliness of this approach led to dependence on outside funding sources for production underwriting. Such sources usually agreed to support projects that further their own agenda. Thus, some of the courses produced served only narrow interests, not the broader ones of adults looking for nontraditional ways to satisfy lower-division degree requirements. The products may have been praiseworthy enough as television. Collectively, however, they added up to little more than a grab bag of discrete courses, rather than a curriculum.

The irony is that UMA officials ignored some of the findings of their own research — the following, for example: ". . . most adult learners want television-based courses, but do not want to feel that they are being entertained or want to have their time wasted."[12] Despite this, they devoted scarce funds to lavish productions that their real constituents did not want or feel they needed. In addition, even though audiences reported that they wanted courses that helped them satisfy credentialing requirements, too often UMA produced TV courses that were of little or no interest to the credentials-driven, time-pressed adults who, as project after project has demonstrated, were drawn to nontraditional study.[13] In a sense, then, UMA goals were thwarted by the benefactors who encouraged them to produce courses that did not address the known needs of their target audience.

OTHER PROJECTS

There are other media-based open or distance learning projects worthy of attention, but to describe them in detail would lengthen this book unnecessarily. We shall restrict ourselves to brief comments on several that typify important areas of activity in television-based instruction: one project that hopes to exploit the potential of the TV medium to realize egalitarian educational goals, and two or three others in which providers of media services work with educators in distributing instructional programming.

The To Educate the People Consortium was developed at Wayne State University in Detroit, with strong support from labor unions that saw in the project study opportunities tailored to the needs of blue collar workers. TEP, like other similar projects in the United States, is not an autonomous credit-awarding institution, but is a consortium of two- and four-year colleges around the country. The instructional system is comprised of print materials supplemented by TV programs (many of them talking-face lectures), weekly in-class discussions, and occasional weekend seminars. The curriculum is interdisciplinary and is designed to be relevant to the kinds of life experience most working adults bring to formal education.

Likewise deserving of notice are regional associations like the Southern Educational Communications Association (SECA) or the Central Educational Network (CEN), which have as goals, "working with colleges and universities" in their regions "in providing an educational alternative to meet some of [adult] learner needs."[14] The function of such media services is to supply video courses for the institutions within regions that make up their memberships. Courses selected by the members are played on public television or cable TV stations, and members accept enrollments in them.

Some cable TV operators also feel that, by giving home viewers access to formal educational opportunities, they enhance their chances of increasing the number of subscribers. One, a cable system based in Denver, Colorado, has established the "Mind Extension University." Several other cable systems, which together reach 1.5 million households of subscribers, as well as homes equipped with satellite receiving dishes, also carry this instructional service. Mind Extension Services have a wide repertory of television courses, and are licensed to carry telecourses distributed by the Public Broadcasting Service's Adult Learning Service, the nation's principal distributor of televised college-level courses. Viewers who want to earn college credit for the courses do so by registering in Colorado State University, to which institution they mail correspondence exercises and through which they take examinations and receive grades.[15]

QUESTIONS OF QUALITY

As was only to be expected, the development of nontraditional projects employing television or other telecommunications technologies has made state higher education agencies uneasy, especially when some service areas go beyond state boundaries. In spite of the minimal impact made on the mainstream of higher education by projects of the kind just reviewed, there have always been talk and apprehension about the possibility of "Universities of the Air" that would be operated by cable TV impresarios with considerable capital reserves but without much legitimate educational control. The educational products resulting therefrom might be substandard or bogus. Such a prospect, understandably, alarms regional and state accrediting agencies.

An investigation of the implications of telecommunications-based long-distance teaching was undertaken by two national organizations concerned with accrediting postsecondary instruction. Their acronyms alone make a significant addition to the already formidable Washington, D.C., alphabet soup of bureaus and associations: the Council on Postsecondary Accreditation (COPA) and the State Higher Education Executive Officers (SHEEHO).

Of most interest to readers of this book, perhaps, is what occasioned the study, which was funded by an office of the U.S. Department of Education. The project directors felt that by 1982, when the request for funding was submitted, there had been a confluence of two significant developments. The first was a "sudden breakthrough in the development of high-quality telecommunications-based instructional materials," which was being brought about by the much-publicized Annenberg/Corporation for Public Broadcasting Project, which established "a stable funding mechanism" for the production of television and other telecommunications-based instructional programs. (The Annenberg/CPB Project, which will be discussed later, established a fund of $150 million to be used over a fifteen-year period to produce media courses and explore the higher educational potential of the new telecommunications media.) Another development prompting the funding request was the fact that, although at one time only open-broadcast television was available for delivering programs, "there is now a plethora of technologies available." Cable, microwave transmission systems, Direct Broadcast Service (DBS), and satellite relay systems "enable an originating institution or organization to feed its programming to virtually any PTV station or cable system throughout the nation at minimal cost."[16]

The question of insuring and maintaining academic quality in off-campus instruction is a real one. Potentially even more vexing are possible legal issues associated with instruction delivered electronically to a given state from outside. What could be the real or fancied bad effects on the instructional programs of institutions within the state? There is also the question, for example, of whether a public university should recognize professional courses offered to citizens of its state on cable television by a university from outside the state, especially when the courses are available from the in-state university.

In any event, this is hardly the place to venture answers to questions of this kind, nor, in fact, have serious legal problems arisen. As for televised courses used nationally, colleges and universities, as well as accrediting agencies, have been doing essentially what the investigators of the project just cited recommended. That is, the best guarantee of the validity and quality of a TV course presented on public television through the Adult Learning Service is the reputation and accreditation standing of the institution that produced the course and the institutions that grant students credit for successful completion of it.

Concern on the part of state and other accrediting boards still persists and is likely to continue, although few states have guidelines or policies addressed specifically to television and telecommunications-based instruction. One agency that has issued a set of guidelines, however, is the Coordinating Board of the Texas Colleges and Universities, which did so in 1984. This policy statement requires that all courses offered "through televised instruction" must "apply" to already approved degrees or certificates. In addition, televised courses must "include print materials and live interactive sessions with the instructor of record." The guidelines go on to stipulate that the live meetings of students and instructors of record must include one or more orientation sessions at the start of a term and periodic sessions conducted either as tutorials or in group settings.

The first part of the provision, the requirement that there be "printed materials," seems almost unnecessary, since it is hard to imagine a college-level course, no matter how presented, without readings or exercises of some kind. The second part prescribing "live interactive sessions" betrays a lingering distrust of television supplemented only by printed materials as an instructional medium. Therefore, the Texas officials feel that students studying at a distance from campus must have an opportunity to meet and confer with the teachers who grade their performance.[17]

Accrediting agencies are certainly to be commended for their efforts to prevent abuses. The multiplication of and the steady reduction in cost of video and other technologies are presenting institutions of all kinds with opportunities to offer their services to adults outside classrooms. There is always the possibility that the unscrupulous will take advantage of the technologies available to present shabby or inferior materials.

PROBLEMS OF PROGRAMMING

The fact remains, however, that, except for certain continuing professional education groups, the nation's reputable colleges and universities, other than some two-year community colleges, are not making the most of the extension possibilities posed by cable television or microwave and satellite linkages. Even when college extension divisions do ask cable operators for time on public service channels, they often make little programming available. Ambitious plans made for statewide or regionwide satellite or cable networks soon come to nought when the colleges involved become aware that there is not enough material to program the service on a continuing basis.

In summary, the early efforts of instructional users of television can remind one uncomfortably of what the American writer Henry David Thoreau once said about men's inventions in general, which "are wont to be pretty toys, which distract our attention from serious things." In his day, men were busily trying to build a magnetic telegraph network to link the country, but as Thoreau commented, "Maine and Texas, it may be, have nothing important to communicate."

Today's educators have marvels of distribution at their fingertips, but like Maine and Texas in Thoreau's day, as yet they do not have enough messages of importance to communicate to make effective use of the marvels. We must admit, in the jargon of telecommunications, that we have a wealth of "hardware" but a dearth of "software." We have at our disposal the means of delivery, but we need more of the right kinds of instructional materials to deliver to audiences. Nor as yet have we been able to design the organizational structures that can make using television for instruction more than a marginal enterprise in higher education.

The Telecourse

ON THE WAY TO A NEW TEACHING METHOD

Adversity has helped the development of what has come to be known as the telecourse. As its designers insist, the telecourse is more than a televised course, much more, that is, than a video recording or live telecast of an instructor teaching as he or she does in the conventional classroom. From the earliest days of instructional television, it has been clear that pointing a camera at a lecturing professor standing at a blackboard or behind a lectern is far from tapping the instructional and motivational potential of the medium. This is not to imply that students watching "talking-face" professors do not learn. As indicated earlier, we know that thousands of well-motivated adults who took Chicago TV College courses learned as much as their peers sitting in conventional classrooms. We know, too, that the graduate engineers who enroll in National Technological University TV courses, which are extensions of the classroom, learn as well as their peers sitting in graduate school classrooms across the country.

However, all students, no matter what their degree of motivation or maturity, welcome production finesse in TV programs, accustomed as they are to the entertainment values of commercial television. Indeed, no matter how highly motivated and eager to learn viewers may be, clumsy TV presentation can distract them and even dampen their enthusiasm. We know, too, from our experience with closed-circuit television on campuses that amateurish production can deter younger students and sour them forever on the medium as a vehicle for instruction.

Effective telecourse producers do not forget also that human interaction is essential in learning for most people. For this reason, purely documentary approaches in video programs, without a visible teacher presence, whether in the form of a real or a convincing actor, do not appeal to some telecourse producers and students who deem a teacher figure essential to establish "one-on-one" contact. Successful telecourse designers are also well aware that allowances must be made for live face-to-face contacts between support teachers and students. A memorable *New Yorker* magazine cartoon makes it clear, as only pictorial representation can, that technology is no substitute for the live encounter. The cartoonist shows a little girl lying in her bed, looking glumly at a TV set resting on a stand nearby. The image on the set is coming from a videocassette recorder. Visible on the screen is her father holding a book and saying, "Pleasant dreams . . . and here's Daddy with one of your favorite bedtime stories."[1]

Educators often deplore some public broadcasters' lack of enthusiasm for instructional programming, as is evidenced by their unwillingness to schedule instructional programs during prime viewing hours. Yet this balking at videotaped classroom lecturing has proved a blessing in disguise. It has forced instructional TV designers not only to try to make their programs more appealing, but also to explore the distinctive properties of the medium that can make it even more effective for teaching.

In addition, as indicated earlier, at the very time much instructional television was being derided as "radio with pictures" or "talking heads," the new instructional technologists and designers were making their appearance. These are professionals, as already noted, who are trained in more than audiovisual methods, but are knowledgeable about learning theory, the analysis of learning tasks, and the combining of human and technological means to achieve learning goals. People with this kind of background serve as members of BOU course preparation teams. People with like training are also members of the course teams designing materials for the prominent community college producers and distributors of nationally marketed telecourses — Dallas, Coast, and the Southern California Consortium. Their stated objective is to design a systematic and systematized kind of learning suitable for adults who study at a distance. One community college instructional designer states that she has four purposes. The first is "to select appropriate instructional strategies for the target audience." A second is to formulate the goals of the course in terms of what a student must demonstrate upon successful completion. A third is to make sure that the course components — that is, the video, the print, and whatever else — are coordinated and mutually supportive. A fourth is to assure that the course content is accurate and free of bias.[2] The results of the design process, the telecourse, has been described as:

> . . . much more than a course on television. It is a learning system, with each of its components, whether video, audio, print, other media, complementing the others and offering students a genuinely new kind of learning experience.[3]

The less tradition-bound adult educators immediately welcomed the telecourse as an exciting alternative way of extending and enriching learning for adults. Unfortunately, such institutional television is expensive, so expensive that economy of scale comes into play, dictating that it must be distributed to broad markets to be cost-effective. Thus, the necessity of adaptability for use by many institutions in different parts of the country also affects the design of telecourses. They must be designed so as to allow users to modify them without too much trouble to suit their own purposes and institutional practices.

Early Telecourse Design

Community colleges were among the earliest continuous users of telecourses in U.S. higher education. Readers acquainted with two-year community colleges and their goals can readily appreciate why this was so. They are expressly committed to serving all segments of their communities, not just those of normal undergraduate age and background. They are less tightly compartmentalized in organization and, in general, tend to be less hidebound in their procedures than are four-year colleges and universities. Thus, many of them are receptive to trying new modes of instruction that can reach out and serve nontraditional kinds of students. Four-year colleges and universities, often comprised of departmental fiefdoms, are adept at shunting the unconventional off to extensions or other divisions and subdivisions, which, at best, are separate but not equal within the institution when matters such as transfers of student credit to regular academic departments are involved.

It will surprise no one, therefore, to hear that community colleges were among the first to standardize a nationally marketable instructional package known as the telecourse. In the early 1970s, several series that established the format appeared. One called *Man and Environment* was produced and designed at Miami-Dade Community College, an institution strongly committed to technological instructional approaches. The topic was selected after lengthy investigation of the need for and marketability of such a course. At that time, concern about preserving the environment was beginning to mount, especially among the younger and better-educated parts of the population. The TV programs, most of them fast-moving documentaries, were designed to appeal to general viewers rather than to students with scientific backgrounds or orientations. A specially prepared text and a student study guide made the series usable for direct instruction. Despite its trendiness and superficialities of treatment, *Man and Environment* was a refreshing change and presaged a new direction for college-level instructional television. Instruction and entertainment had been joined.

In the same year, Coastline Community College of Southern California produced a telecourse in introductory psychology entitled *As Man Behaves*. The goal, as in Miami, was to produce a telecourse that could be marketed nationally and justify thereby the high costs of production and design. The subject of the course, psychology, is as popular with general viewing audiences as it is with the college population. The television programs were produced by professionals, and incorporated on-location film segments, animations, dramatizations, and interviews with internationally known psychologists. The course also included a widely used textbook, available through commercial publishing outlets and specially adapted for the TV course. Also made available were a student study guide and study exercises. Further, adopters of the telecourse were encouraged to schedule face-to-face meetings of local support instructors and students, in addition to telephone conference hours during which viewers could reach instructors.

Interestingly, British Broadcasting Corporation (BBC) programming played a part in the development of the telecourse in the United States, just as it plays an important, indeed indispensable, part in programming U.S. public television. Two BBC series in particular, *Civilisation,* featuring the art historian Sir Kenneth Clark and *The Ascent of Man* with the polymath Jacob Bronowski, demonstrated how television and print materials can reinforce each other and make for rewarding and pleasurable learning. When these series were aired by PBS stations in 1974, staff at Miami-Dade Community College, Coastline Community College, and the University of California Extension at San Diego recognized that these general-audience productions could also be employed for formal, credit-bearing instruction. After discussions, BBC officials agreed to let the colleges produce study materials to supplement the books written by Clark and Bronowski to accompany their video programs. Thus, the "wrap-around" telecourse came about, with its TV programs and specially written books (which include the scripts of the TV programs) supplemented by a student guide, study exercises, and whatever else a user institution may provide.

This may be an appropriate place for what to some readers will seem a digression, but the digression may be excused in that it raises an often hotly debated and relevant question. Telecourses of the kind just mentioned and others that followed raised concerns in the minds of some well-meaning observers as to how far TV producers could go in courting general audiences until they began to dilute or compromise formal instruction. In other words, are instructional and entertainment goals reconcilable? Can all academic subjects be treated so as to appeal to the general audiences TV station managers feel they must cultivate?

These concerns stem in part from reservations some critics have about television as a medium for disseminating ideas. As one observer comments, "It is very difficult to present substantive material in . . . television programs."[4] Producers discover that TV programs of an accounting course designed to be lighthearted and entertaining only distract and annoy serious, mature students, or producers of an introductory economics telecourse find that as many students as are amused and helped by the soap opera story line of the video programs are irritated and distracted. The effects of these mighty efforts to entertain can be, according to some critics, similar to what the Roman poet Horace called the mountains laboring to produce a mouse, a lot of fuss and fury to produce nothing of value.

The Telecourse as a Learning System

As said earlier, its producers and designers remind us constantly that a telecourse is not to be thought of as a college course on television. The TV programs, as large a course component as they may be, are not the sole purveyors of information, the sounding boards for ideas, or the only intellectual stimuli. The typical telecourse now available for college use through the PBS Adult Learning Service is much more than a series of informative TV programs. Rather, it is a combination of video, print, correspondence, and face-to-face activities. When well designed, each element reinforces the other. The video arouses students' interest, helps them mark their progress through the course, brings the outside world into the lessons, involves them emotionally, and exerts a powerfully effective force. The printed materials supply information, analyze in depth, synthesize, test progress and mastery, and so forth. The outcome for a student, the instructional designer hopes, is an experience, on the one hand, much richer than that of the old-fashioned correspondence course and, on the other, much different from that of the conventional classroom, even though it is the equivalent in measurable learning outcomes.

Video

This is, of course, the most "visible" part of the telecourse. It is also the part whose function is most frequently misunderstood. Many academics regard the video program simply as a surrogate classroom experience for a distant student. In the earliest years of instructional television, some faculty even insisted that the number of hours of video instruction must approximate the number of hours spent in a conventional classroom if the TV course were to be regarded as an equivalent of an on-campus course. However, as "talking-face" programs yielded to programs that employed the rhetoric of TV production — visualization, skillful camera movement, in short, showing rather than telling — the insistence on matching "video" time with student "seat" time weakened. Nowadays most telecourses presented on the PBS Adult Learning Service, for example, contain from twenty-six to thirty half-hour programs. The Annenberg/CPB Project, which, until it suspended operations in 1989 because of questions as to its tax-exempt status, was the biggest single source of expensively produced telecourses, sometimes allows for thirteen video programs, each almost an hour in length. This format eases scheduling problems for the PBS stations that present Annenberg/CPB courses on open broadcast. The twenty-six to thirty half-hour program sequence also is easier for stations to schedule within a time frame approximating a college or university academic term.

Aside from easing scheduling for TV station managers, is there any other reason for making twenty-six to thirty half-hour programs the standard for a three-credit-hour telecourse? The reason, as already suggested, has little or nothing to do with questions of instructional effectiveness. Rather, it has to do with improving the marketability of an expensive course. To have any chance of recouping its investment in a telecourse, the producer institution must find as wide a market as possible. Users must have access to air time available if they are to lease telecourses. They can find time more readily if a series of programs can be accommodated to a station's schedule without too much trouble. A standardized number of half-hour programs that can be played weekly over a period of time corresponding to a quarter or semester pose less of a problem than courses with varying numbers of programs that do not fit neatly into a programmer's grid.

We shall see more telecourses with fewer than twenty-six to thirty programs or thirteen hour-long programs within the next few years, however. In fact, BOU designers have for some time been reducing the proportion of video in their courses. One reason, of course, is the soaring costs of video production. Another is that the number of programs appropriate varies from course to course. Certainly, if instructional TV producers' dependence on public broadcasters for distribution of their courses breaks down even more than it already has, there will be less need for the current high proportion of video, particularly as instructional designers make wider use of media other than video to supplement instruction — audiocassettes, the personal computer. In addition, as videocassette recorders (VCRs) become even less expensive and appear in smaller formats, we can look forward to a formal marriage of print correspondence courses and television. A video-related correspondence course in Business Management might very well require only three or four video programs that illustrate certain concepts and procedures, as well as several supporting audiocassettes, plus exercises for the personal computer (PC).

This is not the place, however, to conjecture as to what the future will be like. That shall be done in the last chapter. For now it is more appropriate to consider the production styles we see in the video programs of telecourses now in wide use. Nationally marketed telecourses at the introductory general education level try, within their budgetary limits, to make the most of the special presentational and affective properties of the medium. This means usually that producers employ generous portions of existing film, simulations, dramatic skits, and guest interviews. When done skillfully to achieve predefined goals — using film or simulations to encourage inference-making, for example — all this can result in a distinctive admixture of instruction and delight. If, however, the various techniques are used simply for their own sakes, to add excitement, they may actually impede learning for serious students.

U.S. producers of the telecourses that find national markets, unfortunately, are not always given to self-scrutiny as to their reasons for adopting certain production approaches. Too often, one suspects, they are guided by what will make their materials most attractive not to students, but to station managers. They do not ask themselves often enough what teaching functions specific video techniques can best perform. The BOU, which is not so much at the mercy of broadcasters for air time (although it does experience its share of tension and struggle between BBC producers and academics), through its Audiovisual Media Research Group has sponsored investigations of the particular teaching chores best suited to video and other media.[5] Unfortunately, the instructional effects of media prove resistant to precise assessment. Researchers are all in agreement that, of all the mass media, television is the most powerful and has an effect on learning, these effects varying with the viewer's age, aptitude, educational background, and the subject matter being taught.[6]

Professorial hedging and qualifying aside, however, there can be little argument about the properties that make television effective as an instructional medium. It gives everyone the best seat in the house; it enlarges the smallest object; it is literally a window on the world, bringing the most remote places directly to the student wherever he or she may be; it never tires, but repeats processes and sequences on command until the viewer understands. However, for some tasks it is ineffective. It is not good, for example, for displaying illustrations and graphics that require wide eye span. More importantly, some educators contend that continued viewing of noninteractive, or one-way, video encourages passivity in learners. This is one reason for the growing interest in interactive, or two-way, video among some instructional TV specialists.

A real tribute to television's effectiveness, however, is that "dropout" or attrition rates among telecourse students are usually lower than in old-fashioned correspondence instruction. While he was the BOU vice-rector, Walter Perry always contended, in justifying the high costs of TV production, that TV programs pace a student's progress through a course. A serious student in the classroom gets the most out of his or her class attendance by completing carefully beforehand all the readings prescribed and doing whatever exercises are recommended. The TV program is not unlike the classroom session in that it is most meaningful to the student only if he or she has done all the readings and exercises recommended. In addition, just as every conscientious student feels an obligation to attend every class, even though attendance may not be required, so too the telecourse student feels an obligation to watch every video program.

Perry and his BOU colleagues also argue that the seemingly disproportionate cost of television as only a single element of the independent study mixture can be justified in another way. That is, the video programs give people studying in isolation a sense of community with their fellows studying the same way. Usually, men and women enrolled in television-related independent study programs have only infrequent contacts with teachers or students. The video program is a classroom surrogate in that it imparts a sense of "togetherness" and makes the student feel a part of a common endeavor.

The TV programs can supply a sense of human contact in still another way. Even though today's sophisticated instructional TV producers avoid talking heads in their presentations, they are often prudent enough to employ a host, a real professor or an actor who comes across as one, to control the program's flow and become the viewer's personal guide through the course. Experienced practitioners know that viewers, especially credit students, feel much more secure if a knowledgeable authority figure appears at key moments in a program — to introduce a new topic, to explain a concept, to summarize, or to pull together materials. An unpublished study conducted over a dozen years ago, one that did not receive the attention it deserved in instructional TV circles, showed that telecourse credit students prefer courses that combine straightforward, didactic styles with nondidactic approaches to courses made up entirely of the latter.[7]

Printed Materials

The video program is the highlight of a telecourse, which is understandable since programs, especially when broadcast on open television, are there for all to see. But printed materials comprise an essential element. Students cannot be successful in telecourses unless they do the required readings and carefully follow the instructions in the student study guide. As a matter of fact, students occasionally report that they made respectable grades in telecourses without having watched the video programs.

As in many lower-division college and university courses, a primary textbook is prescribed in most telecourses. Sometimes a second text is required, often a book of supplementary readings to accompany the primary text. In passing, we should note that the currently high cost of books, like the cost of tuition, is a factor that can and does inhibit credit enrollments in telecourses. Telecourse administrators, accordingly, make every effort to keep the costs of textbooks and other materials to a minimum. Texts, as a rule, are available through normal publishing channels and can be obtained through the college or university bookstore in person or through the mail. Publishers of texts that accompany widely used telecourses sometimes adapt their books to the needs of the television students. This happens if the subject of the course is one in high student demand — introductory psychology, U.S. history, national government. Not only do these publishers include inserts relating to the TV programs, but they also publish the study guides prepared for the TV student.

Another essential print ingredient is the student study guide, a kind of publication familiar to anyone who has worked with independent learning programs. The guide requires careful preparation, since it is an indispensable aid to the student who is on his or her own. Ideally, it leads a student through the course, step by step, summarizing what has gone before and signaling what is to come. It contains previews, overviews, and study tips as well as glossaries of terms. It explains correspondence assignments, suggests optional ones, and may contain test items and suggestions for further reading. In recent years, study guides have become increasingly attractive publications, especially when, as indicated above, they are designed and printed by the publishers whose texts are prescribed. Whenever polled as to the usefulness of the various elements of a telecourse, students regularly rate the study guide highly.

Designers show considerable ingenuity in providing study aids for telecourse students. For an art appreciation course, for example, individual kits of slides or prints are put together. For business and computer courses, students are given materials that they use to simulate hands-on experience. The BOU even distributes home laboratory kits to students enrolled in science courses, a practice not likely to catch on in this country because of the likelihood of personal injury suits against sponsoring institutions in the event of accidents.

Major telecourse producers and distributors also publish administrator and faculty guides. Their purpose is to orient faculty and administrators in colleges and universities adopting the courses to them. Instructors recruited to supply local support instruction often are not familiar with independent study procedures. Local coordinators of telecourse activities are often unaware of the kinds of support distant learners must have available to them.

Besides apprising faculty in particular of the special needs and problems of distant learners, these guides also contain samples of the bulletins and communications that must be sent out to distant students in the course of a term. They often contain helpful suggestions as to how telecourse programs can be promoted in the community. Local administrators and support instructors coming to telecourses for the first time find a publication of this kind helpful indeed.

Correspondence and Examinations

Most college-level courses require some kind of written work from students, even if it only takes the form of completing objective tests at mid term and at the end. The amount of correspondence required of telecourse students varies with the nature of the course. Whatever it may be, essays, reports on books or activities, it usually is submitted through the mail. In light of contemporary telecommunications technologies, however, we must think of correspondence as including computers and fax machines. So-called "electronic" mail enables students to transmit messages over telephone lines via their personal computers and modems to an instructor's PC or to those of fellow students. The Annenberg/CPB Project has funded a demonstration project in which students enrolled in a political science telecourse (also funded by The Project) employ PCs to link up with an electronic mailbox. The linkage has a variety of uses: student testing, student conferences with an instructor, and leaving messages for the instructor or fellow students. Investigators are trying to determine if the electronic mailbox can improve a telecourse student's performance enough to warrant the additional costs. Some institutions, too, it should be noted, employ the computer to correct students' exercises, supply tutorial help, and monitor their progress through the course.[8]

Despite the miracles of modern communications technology, old-fashioned correspondence remains and will remain an integral part of learning at a distance, if only because of the expenses of electronic communication, telephone line charges, in particular.

Face-to-Face Meetings

First of all, we must remind ourselves that there are distant learners who can succeed without live contacts with teachers and fellow students. Yet, such students are rare. After all, ideas by their very nature demand to be shared. Therefore, telecourse designers and administrators agree that all students studying at a distance from campus should have regular access to teachers. Even if they have no ideas to share or bounce off someone else's mind, they have a need for information, encouragement, and occasional help. Colleges offering telecourses schedule on-campus conferences, during which students can meet with their support instructors. They also encourage students to telephone support instructors if they have questions or comments. Some go so far as to require that support instructors publish schedules of telephone conference hours, just as they maintain office hours for conventional students. Others, ones with large telecourse enrollments, even maintain telephone "hot" lines that distance students are invited to call at any time. Colleges that are successful users of telecourses do more than schedule conferences. Whenever appropriate, they arrange for students to visit museums in groups, go to the theater, see films, and visit business and industrial sites.

All such activities are left voluntary, of course. Distant educators never forget that some of their students simply cannot avail themselves of the opportunities provided for live interaction. The only on-campus or live meeting that most colleges feel justified in making obligatory is an initial orientation session. These sessions are important, particularly in community colleges where eighteen- and nineteen-year-olds often enroll in telecourses because on-campus classes in the same subjects have been filled. The orientation gives support instructors a chance to alert these generally immature students to the new kind of study on which they are embarking. It was noted earlier that a State of Texas policy statement requires such orientation sessions for telecourse students.

Other Media Components

The open and distance learning projects making the most impact are usually multi-media mixes. BOU students, for example, in addition to video, make extensive uses of radio broadcasts and audiocassettes, as well as computers located in learning centers throughout the United Kingdom. Radio broadcasts are employed for pre-examination reviews, the dissemination of information about activities, and the like. Once again, government control of broadcast works to the advantage of the BOU in that it can claim broadcast time from BBC radio. Thus far, relatively few institutions in this country — the UMA and a number of community colleges come to mind — have become genuine multi-media distance teaching institutions.

Nowadays, instructional designers have a range of nonprint media available to them, from inexpensive audiotapes to expensive computer techniques. Only institutions with large service areas and large numbers of students in telecourses and other kinds of independent study programs are likely to invest in elaborate multi-media support systems.

Other Kinds of Support

As has been said repeatedly, production of telecourses in high-demand undergraduate subjects can come at high cost. To induce insti-tutions to adopt them presupposes considerable time and effort on the part of a number of people. In the first place, someone in the user institution must take the time and trouble to evaluate the content of the telecourse and how well it conforms with the local curriculum. Often the evaluator or evaluators are satisfied that the telecourse is acceptable for use as it is, but at other times, they may feel that it must be adapted to local use. That is, they recommend its adoption only if certain modifications are made in the course. If significant changes have to be made, of course, the telecourse is not adopted. Most changes made by users are by way of adjusting demands made on the student in the course study guide. User institutions also determine how much academic credit should be awarded for successful completion of a telecourse in question, though in most cases they follow the recommendation of the producer institution.

Not until these preliminaries of the local adoption procedure have been completed can a telecourse user decide how much "human" support should be added locally. Telecourses, as already noted, can be managed in a number of ways, through separate administrative units devoted to independent study, or through extensions or evening divisions that handle part-time adult and continuing education programs. Where management responsibility lies, however, is not the key to successful support. Experience shows that successful telecourse programs have certain elements in common. First, they adapt leased telecourses to local settings and give them their own institutional imprint. Second, they make readily available to students extra instructional support and a timely flow of information. Third, they deliver the components of the telecourses at convenient times and places — on cable or open television that students can watch in their homes, on videocassettes that they can view at home, or in other locations at times that suit their convenience.

From what has already been said, it is apparent that user institutions must select local support instructors carefully. Effective support instructors are willing to assume a role somewhat different from the professorial one to which they may be accustomed. They are not the final court of authority classroom teachers like to be. Ideally, they should become senior partners to the students — they themselves should be involved in learning the telecourse content and methodology. In this way, they can anticipate students' problems, and know when further expansions and additional information are needed. The best way a teacher could prepare himself or herself for working with independent study and telecourse students would be to take such a course, and learn what it is like first hand. Perhaps in the future, teacher-training institutions may require prospective college teachers to complete independent study via video or some other media mixture.

The Life of a Telecourse

There remains one aspect of telecourses about which some readers may be wondering. How long is one usable? What is its life expectancy?

To this question, as to so many others, there is no simple answer. The life of a telecourse varies, of course, with its content. It is unlikely that anything will "date," let us say, a telecourse in elementary algebra. The same can be said of, say, an introductory course in geology or earth science, as it is often called nowadays. It is possible, of course, that a new discovery or a startling new hypothesis might render some parts of a course out of date, but the chances are, with one or two of its video programs revised and an updated edition of the textbook employed, the course could stay in use.

Other areas, obviously, are subject to more rapid change. Some subjects in the social sciences, for example, are fairly volatile and must be updated fairly often. On the whole, however, most well-designed telecourses are usable for anywhere for from six to eight years with only minor revisions. We must also keep in mind that some components of a telecourse are easier and less costly to revise than others. Print materials, for example, can be changed with much less trouble and expense than video. A study guide can be revised fairly quickly to reflect a new edition of the textbook to which it is keyed, but video programs are another matter, particularly if several have to be updated or completely redone. That is why TV producers and designers have to be wary of references that date easily, case studies that do not remain exemplary, and so on. One prominent community college producer once presented as an instance of exemplary management in a business telecourse a corporation that went into bankruptcy after the course had been in use for only a few years.

At this point, still another question may arise. Will certain telecourses ever take on the status of classics, or is this an idle question? One can imagine this coming about in areas of aesthetic appreciation where, for example, a master critic considers works of art of enduring value, or, perhaps, an accomplished scientist, who is also an accomplished communicator, presents a memorable series of demonstrations of scientific principles. In any event, the possibility of "classics" emerging is a powerful argument for recruiting eminent scientists, historians, and art critics — provided, of course, they are at ease with the medium — for telecourse presentations.

Forming Higher Education Partnerships

Certainly, questions and doubts have begun to gather in the minds of some readers who have read this far, especially in the minds of ones whose acquaintance with higher education is restricted to its more traditional institutions. Most colleges are best equipped to serve students only in traditional ways — in classrooms, laboratories, and libraries. They are not interested in distributing prepackaged media-based instruction or in producing TV programs — much less in the entertainment business, unless they are involved in big-time sports. Furthermore, where do the colleges that produce and distribute telecourses find the money to produce courses that represent investments of several million dollars? How do they rationalize these costs? Can they really find enough other colleges and universities to lease or purchase such courses so as to recover a substantial part of the original cost? Do not such investments smack uncomfortably of "risk" or "adventure" capital? Then, too, at another end of the scale, how can a college that will enroll only twenty-five or so off-campus students in a telecourse afford to lease a course worth several millions of dollars?

It is feasible for a college or university, with even rudimentary production facilities of its own, or with access at low cost to someone else's, to produce programs and even entire courses for on-campus and local cable TV use or as a supplement to its regular instructional program. However, to involve teams of faculty, instructional design specialists, and TV directors and producers for as long as two years in producing a three-credit-hour course, with camera crews, producer–directors, and academics dispatched to all parts of the country to conduct interviews and gather film footage, is another thing altogether.

Of necessity, television production and use have encouraged a good deal of interinstitutional cooperation in the higher education community, as well as collaboration between the latter and agencies outside the world of higher education. Normally, sharing resources and forming working partnerships with other agencies do not come easily to colleges and universities. How many state education authorities have learned to their dismay that colleges resist cooperative arrangements with other colleges, even when cooperation would mean eliminating needless duplication of facilities and services? On occasion, however, when necessity so dictates, colleges do recognize that cooperation can serve the common good. This is certainly the case with expensive equipment for the physical sciences and telecommunications technologies. Not every university can own and operate the most high-powered telescopes for scanning the skies. Nor can every university within a state system own and maintain the most powerful computers. It is likewise with TV production. Not every institution has the equipment, the personnel, or the financial resources to design and produce instructional TV programs or courses that can be marketed and used nationally.

THE COSTS OF USING AND DESIGNING TELECOURSES

As stated several times earlier, telecourse design can be expensive indeed. Most readers probably have no interest in a detailed analysis of the costs involved in either producing or using a telecourse, but they may be interested in finding out something about the economics of telecourses. At least this information will help them appreciate why growing telecourse use has prompted so many institutions to form partnerships of varying degrees of formality with fellow institutions, public broadcast agencies, publishers, and, in special instances, business and industrial organizations.

The first question a college administrator invariably asks about presenting a course on television is, how much will it cost us? This question is asked so often that the nation's largest distributor of telecourses, the PBS Adult Learning Service, has prepared a brief publication that lists the costs incurred in offering a telecourse.[1] They include the following: (1) licensing or purchasing fees for the telecourses themselves;

(2) salaries for local support instructors and clerical expenses; (3) expenses for student support services; (4) costs of recording and transmitting the video programs; (5) costs incurred for promoting and advertising the telecourse. Unfortunately, licensing fees alone are sometimes enough to discourage colleges, running as high as several thousand dollars for some courses.

Some administrators are momentarily beguiled by telecourses as ways of "making" money, that is, of having tuition revenues exceed expenses. This notion not only upsets faculty members but also deludes its holders. As experience demonstrates, a more sensible attitude to take is that telecourse costs will not significantly exceed those of conventional classroom instruction or, given economy of scale, will be about the same.

The costs of producing a high-quality telecourse that will find use by colleges around the country and appear on public TV stations are beyond the resources of most institutions. According to reports, a currently popular telecourse, *French in Action,* which was underwritten in large part by the Annenberg/CPB Project, cost several million dollars. It was produced on location in France. Such courses are major enterprises, presupposing the skills of academics, instructional designers, producers, cinematographers, directors, writers, actors, and film archivists. Travel costs alone run into hundreds of thousands of dollars.

Some institutions, notably several community colleges, produce such telecourses on their own, always on the presumption that they will recoup their investment by leasing and selling the product to other colleges, not to mention the revenues they will derive from repeated uses of the materials within their own institutional jurisdictions. It seems doubtful that any institution ever completely recovers its original investment. Yet, it can claim as justification the multiple uses to which the materials are put by students on its own campus over the years.

FORMING ASSOCIATIONS AND CONSORTIUMS

When computers were first being introduced into higher education and into business, some people saw that it often made no sense economically to try to acquire full services on their own. Services could often be shared by colleges and businesses with no loss of efficiency and at much lower cost. Not perhaps so quickly, but eventually, colleges and universities also learned that television-based teaching materials can be acquired, designed, and employed in partnership. Partnerships enable institutions, for whom singly the costs of TV instruction would be prohibitive, to share the expenses with others. Such partnerships nowadays are frequently called consortiums, or consortia, whichever plural one prefers.

Colleges join consortia for a number of reasons. The most common are to (1) share resources; (2) make access to products or processes too costly for one member on its own feasible by broadening the user base; (3) bring about more effective design and uses of television and technology-based instructional materials. Just as universities band together to acquire and share the use of sophisticated equipment needed in advanced physics, so too they band together to acquire certain kinds of transmission equipment — satellite "uplinks" and "downlinks," for example, that send and receive TV signals to and from satellites — and television-based teaching materials. The loose confederation of midwestern universities that made up the former UMA all had equal access, among other things, to expensively produced media-based courses, and shared the results of elaborate investigations and surveys of distance teaching procedures and distant learners.

Some TV and telecommunications consortia are regional; others are national. Some are even international, like the International University Consortium, which was described earlier. The two-year community colleges have also formed their own important international consortium of instructional TV and other media users and producers, the Instructional Telecommunications Consortium (ITC). This group, affiliated with the American Association of Community and Junior Colleges, now claims over seventy-five members both in this country and in Canada. Some ITC members are themselves important regional and statewide consortia. Among major ITC goals are sharing information about instructional television and other media, helping members and nonmembers utilize media-based teaching materials effectively, encouraging the cooperative design and production of telecourses and other materials, and furthering cooperative uses by members and others of nonbroadcast TV transmission, especially satellite-based transmission.

The ITC is prominent among associations that concern themselves with broad issues of concern to institutions all across the country (e.g., planning curricula for television-based projects; designing and producing cooperatively widely needed materials; sharing delivery systems). Most other consortia have more narrowly focused interests. One such interest is leasing or purchasing telecourses collectively so as to make their uses feasible for all member institutions, regardless of size. Other groups are committed primarily to sharing delivery systems. One example of this is a New Jersey statewide educational and cultural cable TV network that links all the state's franchises for educational and cultural uses.

Finally, there are partnerships between broadcasters and educators to further the ends of adult distance education. The Learning Channel, a satellite-delivered cable TV service that brings a variety of informal and formal education to cable subscribers, is a notable example of this. At present, the largest broadcast/higher education partnership is the PBS Adult Learning Service, which employs open broadcast, cable television, and satellite transmission to deliver a full schedule of telecourses to colleges and universities every year. These two services will be discussed later in this study.

Acquiring Materials

The one reason that most often moves a college to join a TV or telecommunications consortium is, as indicated above, the desire to gain access to high-quality video materials at a cost it can afford. The PBS Adult Learning Service (ALS), the largest distributor of college video courses, and other distributors negotiate reduced leasing rates with user groups who are members of consortia. This is the practice of collective buying common in business and government. Florida and Oklahoma community colleges and four-year colleges collectively lease or purchase TV materials for use by public institutions within their states. The Florida Department of Education, to cite an example of how such arrangements work, leases a course on behalf of the state's community colleges with the right to record copies of the programs for use within the state. The course to be leased, which is presented on open broadcast, cable television, and in other closed-broadcast modes, is selected by college representatives at an annual meeting devoted to identifying common course needs and screening available materials. These two states are far from being alone in negotiating such collective purchases. There are numerous statewide and regional groups — some of them members of the aforementioned Instructional Telecommunications Consortium — that locate, screen, and acquire telecourses for collective uses.

Cooperative Telecourse Production

Soon after community college producers had introduced the high-quality telecourse, it became apparent that designing such products on a regular basis was beyond the financial resources of just about all institutions on their own. Pooling resources has always been indispensable. Funding from outside sources, whether from branches of the federal government, private foundations, or quasi-governmental agencies like the National Endowment for the Humanities, has always been sought. Until it ceased operations recently, whether temporarily or not is unknown at this writing, the prime outside funder was The Annenberg/CPB Project, whose funds came from the philanthropist Walter Annenberg. Unfortunately, direct funding from the federal government proved to be erratic, particularly once the aura of innovation had begun to wear off instructional television and some of the widely heralded projects supported failed to realize the claims made for them. Occasionally, if a particular telecourse addresses problems of concern to all thinking citizens, support for telecourses may come from business and industrial donors. Business and industrial donors, in fact, often supplemented or matched Annenberg/CPB Project awards.

It is not uncommon for the partners in a telecourse production to be colleges and higher education consortia that share common needs for courses to offer to students studying at a distance. For example, Dallas Community College District, the coordinating producer of *Government by Consent,* a widely used introductory telecourse in American national government, lists the course as produced in association with the following community colleges and associations of community colleges: Coast Community College District, the State of Florida Department of Education, the Higher Education Telecommunications Association of Oklahoma, the Michigan Community College Association, the Northern Illinois Learning Resources Cooperative, and Tarrant County Junior Colleges. One of the partners just mentioned, Coast Community College of California, pioneered this kind of cooperative production. One of the participants is the "lead" or coordinating producer. The actual planning and video production are done at its location, since it has access to or owns professional production facilities and has on its staff instructional designers and TV specialists. The lead institution also is a major financial contributor to the project, since it underwrites a major portion of the production costs and will itself make extensive use of the resulting telecourse. The associates each contribute agreed-upon sums to the effort, as well as the services of faculty specialists who take part in the course content planning. The coordinating producer — Dallas in the case of the National Government telecourse — reserves the right to market the finished product nationally. The associate institutions are granted the right to make unlimited uses of the resulting telecourses within their own educational venues.

Book publishers are sometimes partners in cooperative telecourse productions, as one was to some extent in the Dallas National Government course. In the 1970s, some publishing houses felt it would be to their advantage to be directly associated with telecourse productions. A few even invested their money in the planning. They felt that just having one of their textbooks named as the book to accompany the video programs would result in significantly greater sales. They also thought — somewhat prematurely, as it turned out — that they could market independently certain video programs to supplement the printed text. In any event, disappointing initial experiences led them to withdraw from further significant direct investments in telecourse production. One can only infer that effects on book sales did not warrant the optimism. Probably, too, they discovered that video materials cannot be marketed as are books, which are consumable items. Undoubtedly, there were other reasons as well, one perhaps being that it may be imprudent for a publisher, especially a major one, to become associated with a single institution or group of institutions. All this does not mean, however, that in the future videocassettes will not be designed so as to complement textbooks — and be packaged along with the books for sale to students.

Cooperative design and production are desirable for a number of other reasons. The now suspended Annenberg/CPB Project, which funded telecourse production with a princely hand, wisely insisted that any project it supported have support from other sources. This is the policy of other foundations as well. Put in simple terms, a project is better for representing a pooling of resources from a number of institutions. Thus, a telecourse's shape and content will not reflect the views of a single agency or institution, but the views of experts from various parts of the country. It does not follow that a course will not strongly reflect the approach of the host or the coordinating institution, especially if the host and the coordinating school are prestigious. Nor does it follow that a course will be better or more successful. However, it does allow, for example, an Annenberg/CPB Project–supported course in introductory psychology, created and hosted by a psychologist from a first-rate university, to be promoted as having been produced in association with the American Psychological Association — all of which is equivalent to a Good Housekeeping Seal of Approval or a limited warranty.

Special Service Consortia

Consortia are also formed to render services to special professional groups. These groups often have as sources of their support business and corporate partners. Stanford University was among the first universities to transmit advanced-level engineering, technology, and mathematics instruction to corporate sites. The courses go out live from Stanford classrooms via low-power instructional television fixed service (ITFS) to locations in the Bay Area where engineers and other professionals view them and earn graduate credit for successful completion. The high technology companies involved in the service also have the right to record the transmissions at receiving sites and use the recordings later with students unable to watch live sessions.

To participate in the program, a company must purchase the special receiving antennas and signal converters needed to adapt ITFS broadcast for reception on standard TV monitors. They also pay annual membership fees to the university, which are used to support the project. Given the strong motivation of the students, whose tuition fees typically are paid by their employers, there is no need for production that meets commercial broadcast standards. A professor is on camera as he or she is teaching students in a classroom. All that is necessary is that the professor be a skilled presenter of the material and that the visual aids that are employed be clear. As already indicated, the more advanced the subject matter and the higher the motivation of the students, the less urgent the need for production quality. As noted earlier, mature students enrolled in telecourses at even the introductory level can become impatient with the lack of direct instructional flow in a telecourse like the expensively produced *The Write Course,* an Annenberg/CPB Project–supported course in English composition, or a course in introductory economics called *The Money Puzzle,* produced by a community college. Both courses have continuing video story lines in what was arguably a misguided attempt to capture student interest in the fashion of the "sitcoms" on commercial television.

This kind of continuing professional education, which lends itself to low-cost delivery on nonbroadcast television, established itself quickly and is destined to grow. Satellite-based delivery now makes it possible for continuing engineering education to be distributed by a national consortium of universities, the National Technological University (NTU), an association of about twenty-five engineering schools, including some of the country's most distinguished. The satellite transmits NTU's 300 courses to locations across the country. Engineers and technologists employed by the companies subscribing to the NTU service can earn advanced degrees and certificates. Courses are recorded at reception points where the required receivers, or downlinks, are located for later replay or for retransmission on closed-circuit television, ITFS, or cable television. Like the Stanford video programs, the NTU programs are straightforward capturings of professors as they actually teach their classes.

A large proportion of corporations participating in NTU have tuition-supported programs for employees who enroll in courses, which certainly is a tribute to their confidence in the integrity of the project. NTU is serving both employers and employees by assuring the former that their engineers and technologists are improving their skills and staying up to date in professions where knowledge and skills become obsolescent quickly, and by making it convenient for the latter to earn advance credit and certification. The new TV technologies make it possible for busy professionals, with the responsibilities of job, family, and home, to earn masters' degrees by studying in their homes or at work sites. Officials of NTU, which by the way, now grants degrees in its own right, expect it eventually to become a major source of master's degrees in engineering and technology.

Associations of colleges and universities also provide similar services on local and regional bases, especially in areas where similar kinds of businesses and industries are clustered. An example of this kind of service is the Association for Higher Education of North Texas, or TAGER, which employs microwave transmission to extend classroom instruction in a variety of subjects to corporate sites. Thus, nonbroadcast television is enabling colleges and universities and associations of institutions to break down the classroom's walls and reach out beyond campuses to new kinds of students. These new students and the TV technologies that allow the colleges and universities to reach them will take on greater importance if the predictions of some demographers become realities, and population in the United States assumes the shape of an inverted rather than a normal pyramid. That is, there will be fewer young people at the bottom of the pyramid and many more older people at the top. Colleges may very well have difficulty finding enough students aged eighteen to twenty-two to maintain their facilities and services. These new, relatively inexpensive TV technologies may prove attractive ways of recruiting and teaching different kinds of students off campus.

So promising are the technologies that they are prompting plans that seem to some little more than chimeras, but to others dawning realities.

Satellite technology in particular has sparked the imaginations of many. There is currently, for example, a proposal calling for a Global Electronic University, part of "a worldwide educational network" made up of universities, business organizations, students, and workers to be known as the Global University Consortium. The long-term goal of the consortium is laudable, if tantalizingly vague: to "promote a global perception among young people of the wisdom and experience of the world's cultures" in an age when telecommunications are reducing the world to a global village, as Marshall McLuhan told us. Another and more limited goal of the consortium is "creating satellites for exclusively academic purposes."[2]

The satellite, in particular, is making possible for associations and consortia a number of specialized instructional video services, some of them "noncredit" in the sense that they do not allow viewers to earn credit hours that can be transferred into regular academic programs at a later date. A good example, though by no means the only one, is the National University Teleconference Network (NUTN), an association of higher education institutions that employs the satellite-transmitted teleconference for a number of informational and educational purposes, ranging from AIDS education to methods of processing students' records. As its name suggests, a teleconference is a meeting held at a distance via an electronic medium — in this case the video medium. Every day, people all over the country are being linked together by satellite signals, in college and university continuing education centers, in hotel meeting rooms, in chambers of commerce, and on industrial sites. In fact, participants on various continents are brought together for meetings by satellite.

Effective teleconferences are not impromptu performances. They must be carefully planned and produced, or they quickly become redundant and aimless. An organization like NUTN will supply planning and actual production for its members. A typical program pattern is as follows: a formal presentation is made by an expert or a panel of experts in a studio setting. Participants watch in locations where, often, arrangements are made for follow-up discussion involving local experts. Participants usually are free to ask questions of the studio experts via telephone or audio connections.

Organizations like NUTN and other teleconference groups answer a real need in the higher education, professional, and business worlds. For one thing, they allow groups to address common problems in a timely fashion. Suppose, for instance, a change in federal tax laws suddenly makes it necessary for thousands of lawyers and tax accountants to bring themselves abreast of the new legislation, or suppose new legislation in Washington makes it imperative that higher education administrators be briefed on the implications. Fairly quickly, a panel of experts can be convened for a video teleconference originating in Washington, and viewing sites can be set up within a region or around the nation. Arrangements can also be made for follow-up discussions at receiving sites.

Since some teleconferences last as long as several hours, it is understandable, as indicated above, that participants do become bored and inattentive as the proceedings drag. For this reason, the professional teleconference associations — NUTN, the PBS Teleconference Service, the Public Service Satellite Corporation (PSSC), the U.S. Chamber of Commerce's BizNet, to name several — have planning and production specialists on staff to handle the often complex activities and logistics. Teleconference management will undoubtedly become an important telecommunications subspecialty in the future.

Unless radical changes in human nature come about, most people will continue to prefer face-to-face meetings in resort-like surroundings. Yet, the videosatellite can eliminate costly travel expenses, and its talkback capabilities make it the next best thing to the live encounter. It has already wrought significant change in the staff development procedures of institutions and corporations.

Broadcaster/Higher Education Partnerships

It hardly needs saying that, if open and closed broadcast technologies are to be effective ways of delivering instruction, close relationships must exist between educators and broadcasters. Indeed, studies conducted in the past showed that colleges and universities were cooperating, especially with public TV stations, in making direct instruction available to off-campus students. Community colleges were in the vanguard, with more than 30 percent of them offering courses on open broadcast as long ago as 1977.[3]

Despite the collaboration between adult educators and broadcasters, their relationship at times appears to be made up equally of love and hate. Most people understand why commercial broadcasters are cool toward programming that has as its immediate purpose the imparting of knowledge or the teaching of skills. Nowadays commercial broadcasters show scant interest in even broadly informative programs, as is attested to by the scarcity of serious documentaries and the almost complete absence of serious drama on the networks. Discussions of serious issues are shunted off to Sunday mornings.

Since the 1950s, perhaps the salad days of television, when NBC presented Professor Frank Baxter's Sunday Shakespeare discussions and the Ford Foundation helped underwrite *Omnibus,* one of commercial television's high points in cultural service with its mixture of serious drama, music, and ideas, there has been a steady and inexorable regression to the lowest common denominator of public taste. Most Americans would agree that air time on television is too valuable a commodity to be squandered on narrow audiences and specialized tastes. They accept this either as a fact of life or as a national disgrace.

Some people do express surprise, however, when they learn that public broadcasters, still thought of as educational broadcasters by a large part of the general public, are reluctant to schedule telecourses during evening hours, even the products of the Annenberg/CPB Project, which relieve the infrequent appearances of a professor with views of attractive young actors and actresses walking along the Seine or seated at sidewalk cafes. Any program whose aim is to teach something directly — how to make conversation in French, for example — often gets short shrift. To have a chance at prime time showings on PBS, programs should be educational in a broad sense. This is why, perhaps, some educators see a good portion of the Annenberg/CPB courses as only "broadly" educational. A series on the menaces to peace posed by the nuclear age, which revolves around a topic of interest to the thoughtful part of the TV audiences, will be aired at prime time. It is timely, excites strong feelings and partisanship, and it can be handled without any of the stodginess of direct instruction.

By now, it is no secret that the officials and staffs of PBS stations in the country's major markets no longer feel it is their role to aim at the narrow interests of limited audiences interested in formal education. Some flatter themselves that they are transatlantic cousins of their BBC colleagues catering to select tastes. Others even see nothing inappropriate about vying for larger audiences by showing movies without any pretense of artistic or other merit, with the competitive advantage of being able to show films without commercial breaks. However, the absence of commercials soon may be a thing of the past as well, since PBS stations now carry commercial messages from sponsors euphemistically known as "enhanced underwriting." Some of the staunchest well-wishers of public broadcast are beginning to wonder how long it will be until it is no longer the alternative to commercial television that Congress funded it to be, but just another network whose tunes are called by commercial pipers.

Even as the original educational TV stations were being transformed into public TV stations through the good offices of recommending Carnegie Foundation committees and the U.S. Congress, the newly emancipated educational broadcasters started to advise educators eager to present college courses on television to look to cable channels and nonbroadcast television like ITFS as ways to deliver their programs. It seems right, as well as ironic, that in Chicago a second PBS channel, owned and operated by the city's community college system, now promotes itself as the city's "educational" PBS station, offering as it does a schedule of college-credit telecourses and informal instructional programming.

Despite the inhospitable attitude of some PBS stations toward instructional programs, and despite the growth of cable television and the increasing presence of videocassette players in homes and libraries, surveys of telecourse students and their viewing habits still show that between 60 and 70 percent report that they watch courses at home on PBS. Only about 20 percent report that they watch on cable television.[4] How can this anomaly be explained? Perhaps the simplest explanation is that most viewers fail to distinguish between open broadcast and cable. We must also remember that many PBS stations are college or university controlled, a fact that would make attitudes toward direct instructional programming less overtly hostile, though by no means preclude hostility.

The sometimes prickly relationship between higher education and public broadcasting has made both educators and broadcasters uncomfortable at times. The latter cannot entirely avoid materials designed for viewers interested primarily in instructional content. The former, at times left uneasy by the "show-biz" quality and the occasional absence of scholarly detachment in some well publicized Annenberg/CPB Project telecourses, can only grit their teeth and try to force the telecourses into approved or approvable curriculum molds. At times, too, the materials, timely and attractive as they are, seem adult education in the informal Chautauqua sense, rather than the kind of instruction serious distant learners can use to satisfy degree and credentialing requirements.

Public television, however, even though its eye may be on a broader constituency, is nonetheless a valuable ally of higher education. PBS officials have unequivocally welcomed alliances with higher education. This is not altruism pure and simple. A project like the Annenberg/CPB Project has been a source of prime time programming for PBS during a period of financial austerity and seeming dearth of creative talent. This also does not mean that more public TV stations will be offering air time to institutions with telecourses. It should be noted that PBS stations offering air time charge fees for airing the telecourses, ranging typically from $100 to $300 an hour, and often considerably more in major markets.

PBS stations throughout the country stay in touch with higher education by appointing, as Adult Learning liaisons, staff who work with local college representatives in scheduling and promoting telecourses. In addition, PBS now renders colleges and universities extremely valuable services through the newer TV technologies it employs, especially satellite and narrow-cast transmission.

The Adult Learning Service (ALS)

The PBS Adult Learning Service is supported by fees paid by the colleges and universities that lease the telecourses it distributes. Through associated PBS stations, it broadcasts telecourses and related programs to institutions all over the country. Participating colleges accept enrollments, supply whatever local support instruction they deem necessary, and award students credit for successful completion. ALS officials report that more than 1,500 colleges offered ALS-distributed courses between 1981 and 1989. The courses were presented in cooperation with about 300 public TV stations, with enrollments of over 1.3 million students over the 8-year period. A summer 1989 ALS press release projected that more than a quarter of a million students "would have earned college credit during the 1988–89 academic year using telecourses from the Public Broadcasting Services Adult Learning Service." Even after due allowance is made for the exuberance of writers of press releases, there can be no doubt that ALS is providing an invaluable service to adult and continuing education. ALS currently stands as the prime distributor of nationally usable undergraduate telecourses.

The telecourses distributed by ALS come from the country's major producers of college-level courses, including the Annenberg/CPB Project. ALS also maintains an up-to-date catalog of the courses and other video materials it distributes. It transmits to cooperating stations on closed-circuit broadcasts previews of telecourses to be offered during a coming year. In return for its services, a participating college or a group of colleges participating as a unit pays ALS a licensing fee for the right to use its course. Tuition fees are also shared with ALS on a per capita basis.

ALS has also established several auxiliary services. The Adult Learning Satellite Service (ALSS) delivers telecourses and special services directly via satellite transmission to institutions that own or have access to the downlink receivers required for reception. This delivery service enables colleges to license or purchase telecourses or special programs for on-campus instructional enrichment, library holdings, or uses on cable television, open broadcast, or videocassette. It gives colleges several advantages. For one thing, it enables them to cut down on the amount of videotape they buy, since they do not have to acquire a set of tapes to record each course as they do when ordering series from distributors in the normal way. They can recycle tapes already on hand as they record off the satellite. In addition, the recording can be done more efficiently since ALSS transmits its programming in blocks. Block transmission also allows college faculty to sample an entire course before making an adoption decision, instead of relying simply on one or two programs mailed for screening by the distributor.

The September 1989 issue of the ALS newsletter, *Agenda,* reported that nearly 1,000 colleges and universities leased ALSS programs during 1988, its first year of operation. About 30 percent of total ALS telecourse activity in 1988–89 came from colleges participating in ALSS.

Another ALS special project is the National Narrowcast Service (NNS). This special service exemplifies a new kind of cooperation among broadcasters, higher education institutions, and business/industrial training organizations that some observers feel is destined to play a major part in technology-based distance teaching in the years that lie ahead.

The Annenberg/CPB Project funded a fifteen-week demonstration of NNS that ran from February 3 until May 16, 1986. The purpose was to test the usefulness of and the market for specialized programs for adult continuing education and training conducted by colleges, universities, business, industrial, and public agencies. The programs, including two complete college courses in English composition and physics, along with a group of series in management, office communications, and sales, were sent via satellite to public TV stations for off-air videotaping. Later, at convenient times, they were transmitted via microwave or cable television to campuses and work sites. Taping off the air allowed the training directors of the participating business organizations to review and select materials to be used. Participants were assessed nominal fees for taking part in the demonstration. On the basis of the trial, the PBS Board decided to incorporate NNS into its range of regular services.

According to ALS officials, experience with NNS thus far confirms the promise of three-way training/education projects involving public broadcast, business, and industry.[5] Both business trainees and campus undergraduates were enrolled in NNS courses during the trial period. For the most part, the collegiate subscribers were community colleges, which suggests not surprisingly that the two-year institutions, typically more open to nontraditional procedures, are more likely to award academic credit for special courses conducted for business and industrial training groups. Given the demographic and economic changes occurring in the United States as this century comes to its close — and assuming relevant and suitable educational/training materials will be available, a big assumption — such alliances of broadcast technologies, postsecondary educators, and occupational/professional trainers will become commonplace.

As hinted in the preceding sentence, one serious reservation observers have about services like NNS is whether they can produce or otherwise acquire adequate supplies of up-to-date programs to satisfy the training needs of the business community, which often has needs specific to itself. There is also the always recurring question of the level of TV production values if the attention of viewers whose occupations are subprofessional is to be captured. This problem, as we have seen, is one that has plagued instructional TV producers since the early days. Unfortunately, the delivery capabilities of the technologies far outstrip the abilities of designers and producers to generate the programs to exploit the capabilities.

Television and Distance Learning in the United States

THE DISTANCE EDUCATION MOVEMENT

If anything of real significance has been said to this point, it surely is that one of the most exciting uses higher education is making of television is in extending education, literally making the classroom walls fall and reaching out to men and women in their homes, community centers, and work places. It may be helpful, then, to place television-based instruction within the larger context of the worldwide distance education movement, particularly as it affects adult learners.

As indicated in a preceding chapter, the success of the British Open University (BOU) encouraged adult educators in both developed and developing countries to establish distance and open learning systems.[1] We have already seen how some U.S. institutions tried with little success to adapt BOU teaching materials to their own quite different institutional contexts. Despite the bandwagon enthusiasm that led some U.S. educators to ill-advised attempts at direct importation of materials, the BOU example did stimulate productive thought about adult and continuing education and, above all, about the special problems of adult learners. At least, "it . . . prompted many to reconsider previously unquestioned notions as to the form university-level education should take, who is entitled to it, and when in life it should be experienced."[2] That is, is it acceptable any longer that higher education be tailored primarily to the needs of young adults with the leisure to devote all their time to it, even though more and more adults beyond the eighteen- to twenty-two-year-old span now enroll in colleges and universities, most often as part-timers? Why should not institutions actively recruit people at all stages of life and accommodate their programs to the needs and convenience of such students — as indeed some are now doing? Does not accommodation imply the employment of the mass media, especially television, which is so much a part of everyday living in the United States?

European adult educators, especially those in West Germany and Scandinavia, are given to theorizing about distance education and learning, open learning, correspondence education, independent study, and the like. One German authority, for instance, argues that distance education differs in kind from conventional education in that it is "industrialized," that is, it is dependent on the mass production of materials, on a division of labor characteristic of industrial production in preparing materials, and on technological means in reaching large numbers.[3]

U.S. and British distance educators, however, have little taste for precise definitions and theories. The only notable exception would seem to be the late University of Mid-America (UMA) where researchers showed some interest in establishing a theoretical foundation. However, most investigators in the United States and the United Kingdom feel it is enough to regard distance education as distinguishable from conventional education in that its precondition is a separation of students from teachers for part or all of the time. Yet, no matter how down-to-earth or pragmatic one's approach, there are still legitimate questions that pop up as to how the process of distance education differs, say, from reading the Harvard Classics or the Great Books on one's own or as part of a discussion group.

As we have noted, U.S. distance education projects are usually validated or credentialed through established conventional higher education agencies. The BOU and distance teaching universities in other parts of the world are chartered as freestanding institutions, and can validate their own instruction, grant credit, and award certificates and degrees on their own. U.S. counterparts, like the former UMA or the Wayne State University To Educate the People Consortium, lack that authority and must seek their validation through cooperating conventional colleges and universities. Any U.S. television-based or television-related distance teaching system that makes a pretense of offering a distance learner a realistic chance of completing a meaningful portion of a degree program must rest on some sort of consortial base. This is so for several reasons. First, it is, perhaps, the only way to build a large enough population base to make programs for distance learners economically feasible. Second, cooperative arrangements ease raising the funds needed to produce or acquire the repertory of mediated courses needed if a distant learner is to be able to complete a set of degree or certificate requirements within a reasonable time. The burden does not fall on only one institution, but can be shared by a number.

Another disadvantage that U.S. distance educators labor under is that they must adjust their planning to the schedules and deadlines of partners. In this respect, the complaint of a director of an Annenberg/CPB–sponsored demonstration project is typical. He had, he reports, to mesh the schedule of his project with that of his university, complying always with the latter's fixed dates and unchangeable features. In addition, he was forced to make his schedule of operations jibe with that of a corporation supplying the telecommunications equipment for the project. All this had to be orchestrated in such a way so that he could insure that his own project proceeded step by step.[4]

American distance educators, with the exception of those in community colleges, are subject to several masters. A university offering telecourses to students off campus usually enrolls them in an extension division, which itself has limitations imposed on it by regular academic divisions. The latter determine matters as important to students as how much credit earned through the extension can be transferred to degree programs. Thus, distance higher education projects seldom have any life of their own in this country. Outside the mainstream, they survive at the sufferance of other divisions.

In the early 1970s, a period of euphoria for those interested in nontraditional instructional procedures, some adult educators did hope that open learning, as it was then called, would become more than an adjunct to higher education. Those years saw a flowering of plans for independent and open learning. In retrospect, it seems that all this exuberance bespoke a naiveté about the markets of adult learners just waiting to be tapped. According to a survey done by the now defunct National Association of Educational Broadcasters (NAEB), there were some one hundred institutions or programs dedicated to nontraditional learning modes. What substance there was to the programs is another question.

In the same years, individual state authorities commissioned prospectuses for nontraditional and open institutions that would award adults degrees and certificates for study completed in nontraditional ways. All of this made representatives of the conventional higher education establishment uneasy. To take on respectability, electronically based and correspondence courses, proficiency examinations, and real life and work experiences must be translated into standard academic coinage: classroom contact hours, discrete courses, credit hour equivalencies. U.S. distance education has been characterized by the adult educator Charles Wedemeyer as "learning undertaken in a transactional relationship with educational programs and institutions." As he says, such "backdoor learning," or tutelage achieved outside the conventional classroom, is an embarrassment to the educational bureaucrats who are uncertain as to how to turn it into the language of academic transcripts. Wedemeyer goes on to note that American institutions allowing adults to earn degrees in nonconventional ways are forced to serve, in effect, as brokers of academic and quasi-academic experiences. They negotiate with the students themselves to validate their experiences. These institutions are outsiders in higher education. They are the backdoor. If they are considered alternatives, they are regarded as second-rate ones. The bureaucrats just mentioned are obsessed by the instructional process itself, by the "how" rather than by the "what" that results.[5]

Some good things did come out of this nontraditional ferment. There are now programs, some of them affiliated with reputable institutions and associations of colleges and universities, that allow adults to combine formal learning and life experiences to earn degrees. Some of the expressly experimental "open" colleges founded still survive, although some have abandoned experimental approaches in favor of a return to more traditional methods. One notable survivor is the State University of New York's Empire State College, which permits its students to combine individualized study, credit earned elsewhere, and credit earned in unusual ways — through learning contracts between student and tutor, for example — in degree-directed curricula.

TELEVISION AND DISTANCE TEACHING

After all that has just been said about the vicissitudes and handicaps of distance education in this country, it is still obvious that television-based instruction and other kinds of distance teaching methods are making significant impact on higher education, on the community colleges in particular. Since less authority usually resides in departments in the two-year colleges, there are fewer barriers in the way of adopting TV courses and other kinds of mediated courses. The statistics on telecourse enrollment in the community colleges are impressive indeed.

Unfortunately, they do not always give the kind of information we would like to have, such as how many enrollees actually complete their courses and what they do with the credit earned. Some colleges, of course, do try to keep careful records and gather information about dropout percentages and student characteristics.

The need for data of this kind is what encouraged the Instructional Telecommunications Consortium of the American Association of Community and Junior Colleges to undertake its *Telecourse Student Survey,* now in its third year and planned to be carried on as long as support can be found for it. The Annenberg/CPB Project contributed financial support for the first three years. The population studied in the Telecourse Student Survey is, it must be remembered, mostly a community college one. As we have already seen, there is now emerging a population of distant learners who turn to television for advanced training in highly specialized professions. Naturally, we can expect them to differ demographically from adults enrolled in community college telecourses in introductory subject areas.

Opportunities for Distant Learners

Looked at overall, telecourse enrollments are large. The PBS Adult Learning Service reports that about 1,400 colleges and universities offered credit for its courses over a seven-year period, and that over 1 million students have already been enrolled. As this is written, the ALS boasts a catalog of some forty complete courses in the fine arts, humanities, social sciences, science and health, engineering, technology, professional development, and teacher training. Taken in the mass, the enrollments are indeed large, but the fact is that many colleges participating in ALS, as well as users of telecourses from other sources, may enroll no more than twenty-five to thirty students in a course, and offer no more than one or two courses in a term.

Enrollments tend to be clustered in certain parts of the country. At first glance, it may seem surprising that the size of enrollment is not related to the population base. For example, the State of Wisconsin Vocational Technical and Adult Education division, which makes extensive use of video-related instruction in its outreach programs, reported about 3,500 telecourse credit students in its 1986–87 school year. Austin Community College in Texas, despite its modest size, reported 1,500 telecourse enrollments in Fall 1987. Although a large population base may be helpful, it is not an absolute precondition. The Adult Learning Service reports California as its top telecourse enrollment state, with almost 96,000 enrollments from the service's inception in 1981 until the end of 1988. Yet, the same report lists Oregon, certainly not among the country's most heavily populated areas, as second with almost 89,000 enrollees.[6] Undoubtedly, if they are to attract students, telecourses must be vigorously promoted.

Telecourses certainly are attractive to distance learners in that they help them circumvent the problems of time and inconvenience that nag so many adults looking for higher education opportunities. Nonetheless, telecourse programs must be carefully planned and promoted within the college's service area and, above all, must have warm commitment from top-level administrators. The chief administrators of large multi-campus community colleges that enroll thousands of students in telecourses every term — for example, Dallas Community College District and Tarrant Community College District in Fort Worth — are warm supporters of television as a way to bring education to more people. The statewide and regional consortia of telecourse users and the single institutions that enroll large numbers term after term all have staff dedicated to promoting telecourse use. They have learned how to make telecourses attractive and how to deliver them to their constituencies. Some, for example, are tireless in their efforts to persuade cable operators in their communities to give them air time on channels. In the State of Florida, for example, as a result of the efforts of a consortium of schools and colleges formed by the Florida Department of Education, courses are aired on cable channels in some communities twenty-four hours a day. In fact, Florida college telecourse coordinators hope that soon they will be presenting on cable television all the general education courses required for the two-year Associate of Arts degree.

Distant learners in the United States have at their disposal a host of TV technologies — open broadcast television, cable television, closed-circuit transmission, satellite delivery, videocassettes, and videodiscs. These same media give U.S. distance educators a remarkable versatility. Learners are no longer solely reliant on the U.S. mail to deliver study materials to their mailboxes every week, and they do not have to rely on local public TV stations to bring them video programs every week. Nowadays, they can watch a telecourse program on a cable channel that repeats the same program several times during the week, both early and late in the day, or they can watch videocassettes on their video recorders at home. Some even can watch programs where they work or in community centers like public libraries.

The newer technologies have brought still newer clients to higher education. Narrowcast television — microwave transmission, Instructional Television Fixed Service (ITFS) — now allows colleges and universities to deliver college-level instruction to qualified high school students in school districts where there are not instructors qualified to teach them. Chico State University in California and Oklahoma State University, to cite only two, are employing the satellite and microwave transmission to bring foreign language classes, physics, and advanced mathematics to secondary schools. The TI-IN Satellite Network in Texas provides advanced-placement courses in foreign languages, physics, computer science, and algebra to schools in Texas and elsewhere. This network and others are participants in the Star Schools Project, a U.S. Department of Education program established in 1988. Star Schools is a comprehensive program of distance education for the elementary and secondary levels. The four telecommunications associations involved in the project will deliver live and interactive instruction by way of satellite, computer, and videotape to small and disadvantaged schools. Much of the instruction in the project will come from studio-classrooms. Some of the classrooms in which instruction originates will be in cooperating universities, with emphasis on foreign languages, mathematics, and science.

The networking made possible and economically feasible by the newer technologies allowed a sparsely populated state like Maine to develop its Community College of Maine/Telecommunications System, which can deliver community college courses and curricula, continuing professional education, and special services to high school buildings, university campuses, and other sites throughout a large state via fiber optics, microwave, and ITFS. Programs can also be brought directly into homes through the facilities of the Maine Public Broadcasting Network. Where there would otherwise be no community college service or an inequitable distribution of services, there is now the electronic equivalent of one. As a 1989 report by the Office of Technology Assessment, commissioned by the U.S. Senate Committee on Labor and Human Resources (*Linking for Learning: A New Course for Education*) states, "Advanced technological capability at lowered cost increases the options for distance education." The same report sums up the significance of electronic networking in distance education:

Distance education makes feasible the linking of all levels of education — elementary, junior and senior high to higher and continuing education. . . . Distance learning networks that link universities, schools, and informal learning institutions, such as museums and public libraries, lead not only to expanded services but to new relationships.[7]

Higher education institutions employing TV technologies are helping adults of all ages to overcome age-old barriers. As already noted, studies of adults who learn in nontraditional ways conducted all over the world agree that distance, time, age, expense, and fatigue are the most formidable barriers to participation in formal schooling. Expense is the only obstacle that television-based distance education cannot help eliminate, outside, perhaps, the community colleges, where student fees are modest. One day, one hopes, adults enrolled in telecourses may even be eligible for state or federal scholarship aid.

TV technologies, it seems almost unnecessary to add, are having most impact on distance teaching and learning in the developed industrialized nations, particularly in the United States where TV sets, according to reports, are even more common than bathtubs. The videocassette recorder and player is fast establishing itself as a staple item in households of even the most modest means. Cable television is in about half the country's homes, and it may be only a matter of time before it reaches most. Satellite receivers are dotting — or, as some say, disfiguring — the landscape. In addition, personal computers (PCs) are commonplace in homes and schoolrooms. Thomas Edison State College in New Jersey, an institution dedicated to instructional experiment, is already employing a teaching system with distance learners whereby home computers are linked to an instructor's via the telephone. A reputable professional development agency like the American Management Association delivers instruction via this approach through a proprietary organization called Telelearning Systems, As we have seen, the PC is already being combined with television to make learning interactive for the student studying at a distance.

Listing examples of distance teaching strategies made possible by the newer technologies is of little interest and relevance. What is noteworthy is the reciprocal relationship between the newer TV and telecommunications media and the needs of distant learners. In parts of the United States, for example, the necessity of devising ways to bring instructional programs to people of all ages in remote and sparsely populated areas has spurred the development of satellite communications systems. Likewise, special instructional needs have led to the formation of media networks so as to add more versatility to distance education. Thus, the telephone, the computer, and television can be tied together to individualize instruction for the distant learner, not to speak of unlocking a treasure trove of information. One should always take with a large grain of salt the pronouncements of the futurists who keep springing up in our high-technology society, but at times what Alvin Toffler said about "an information bomb . . . exploding in our society" seems restrained.[8]

TELEVISION AND THE HIGHER EDUCATION PICTURE OVERALL

The focus of this chapter has been on the effects of television on distance education procedures. Nonetheless, it seems relevant to comment, if only briefly, on how television as an instructional medium is affecting all of higher education. Its impact has been good — and not so good.

As for the latter effect, the generally unsatisfactory trials of closed-circuit TV teaching have already been considered. Attempts to make television a surrogate for classroom instruction or a way to stretch faculty resources have, in general, not been well received, especially by students of normal college age who will not accept a flickering image on a TV screen as a substitute for the flesh-and-blood figure in the classroom. As also noted, younger students, weaned on slick commercial television, are not yet so hungry for knowledge that they overlook the crudities of much in-house TV production.

Despite the bad taste and distrust left behind by closed-circuit TV teaching, the medium itself is adding much to on-campus instructional experience. Like film, but much easier and more convenient to use, it enriches the classroom and is an invaluable library resource. Programs on videocassettes can be played over cable systems on campus so that students can view them in dormitories, or they can be played on library VCRs so that individual students can watch them.

Besides, video resources are increasing year by year. One cannot imagine a college or university not acquiring the BBC Shakespeare Plays, which present on videocassettes the entire canon of the plays acted by skilled British actors in authentic settings. Anyone who has taught or taken a course in Shakespeare or in drama can appreciate how much the easy availability of such a supplement can add to the student experience and learning. The John and Catherine MacArthur Foundation now makes these programs, and others, available to all public libraries.

Also to be mentioned in this connection is a relatively new combining of book and video as exemplified in series such as *The Story of English,* a history of the development and varieties of the English language, or the Annenberg/CPB Project–sponsored *Art of the Western World,* where text and video programs complement each other and provide a really distinctive kind of learning experience for students working on their own. Complementarity of this kind is also found in the earlier BBC series, *Civilisation* and the *Ascent of Man,* where the accompanying texts are essentially scripts of the TV programs. More recent products of this kind are so designed that video and print closely reinforce each other, with the former illustrating, exemplifying, and elaborating on the latter. This wedding of video with print to enrich learning is a truly remarkable development made possible by TV technology.

The video technologies hold great promise for both conventional and distance learning. If the directors of the world's museums are cooperative, art history students will soon be employing videodiscs and their keypads to call up slides of art works from collections all over the world for display on TV screens. The videodisc, which has a capacity of some 40,000 still frames and employs a microcomputer for the rapid retrieval of the information in the frames, is a real boon for the art history student, as well as for the science student. Among the Annenberg/CPB demonstration projects is one based at the University of Nebraska to determine whether the interactive disc can be used by students as a satisfactory alternative to hands-on chemistry, physics, and biology experiments in laboratories. The project indicates that the interactive videodisc is a satisfactory substitute for the "wet" laboratory. Some teachers of the natural sciences feel that much of the time students now spend in laboratories is unproductive. The video/computer combination just described can be just as effective a way of teaching the scientific method and basic experimental procedures.

Computer technologies, of course, are having a dramatic impact on higher education, as well as on instruction at all levels. The PC, now common on just about all campuses, is an interactive medium that allows for individual pacing. It is being used in just about every department of instruction. Faculty readily become enthusiastic over the computer as an instructional aid. However, according to a 1985 Annenberg/CPB Project report, some faculty also see the video technologies as valuable ways of attacking what they consider problem areas of instruction.[9] Eighty-four instructors from seven colleges were requested to identify major instructional problems. Included in the responses were the following five:

(1) encouraging students to express abstract concepts; (2) motivating students to learn actively; (3) adapting instruction to student differences; (4) encouraging the mastery of generic skills — critical thinking, inferential thinking, and so on; (5) finding materials to use in improving faculty skills. Another group of 173 instructors from eight other colleges and universities said that they considered video, audio, and computer technologies effective ways to combat these problems. In addition, they singled out properties of the media helpful in attacking common instructional problems. For one thing, the media allow students to experience vicariously times and events that cannot be recreated in a classroom or a textbook. For another, they permit students to experience real events without any danger to their well-being and comfort.

Video technologies are helpful in handling all the problems listed above — more useful in some than in others. A program of a telecourse in psychology produced by Coastline Community College, for example, allows the students actually to see researchers carrying out an experiment that is only described in a textbook, or, in another video program, students can see and hear B. F. Skinner as he comments on his own theories. Otherwise, Skinner is just a name mentioned in the textbook. How often, too, do students ever have a chance to hear prominent public figures speaking out on pressing issues in social ethics, as they can in the programs of the Annenberg/CPB Project's *Ethics in America*?

Modern video technology, in short, permits the teacher, with little or no trouble, to make experiences available to students that were never available to them before. A teacher of German can now bring actual, up-to-date newscasts and commentaries from German television into the classroom or into a library learning center. A satellite downlink on the college campus receives the program from the transponder of a satellite orbiting above; time zones are no longer problems. The program can be recorded on videotape and played whenever needed. For that matter, American students of German even exchange views with students in Germany via the marvel of video teleconferencing.

One of the problem areas mentioned above had to do with helping faculty become more effective as teachers, a major concern in many institutions, whether the institutions and their faculties admit it or not. Video teleconferencing is one way for colleges to conduct faculty in-service training on a regular basis. As one might expect, much more of this kind of training goes on in community colleges where teachers are valued more for classroom performance than for research and publication. To cite only a few examples: North Carolina's Community

College officials brought an internationally recognized authority on learner motivation to interested faculty and staff throughout the state via a video teleconference. The American Association of Community and Junior Colleges delivered a seminar on literacy and the work place to nearly 1,000 downlink sites where about 150,000 people were gathered. Among the participants were Mrs. Barbara Bush and other public figures. Follow-up discussions were carried on at the receiving sites under the direction of local experts on problems of adult literacy.

Video teleconferencing is finding extensive uses among professional continuing education groups. The American Bar Association sponsors an annual schedule of conferences for lawyers and others concerned with legal matters. Law school professors, government lawyers, and experts in corporate law make presentations that are received in locations around the country. Audiences are invited to interact via telephone or audio connection.

Respondents in the faculty survey that has been discussed also alluded to instructional problems arising from individual differences in students. Television — in particular the presence of TV production facilities of some kind on many college campuses — encourages energetic teachers to produce video materials on their own, or acquire materials from outside sources, that help students with their course work. Some colleges and universities with in-house TV systems use them to deliver special instructional programs and review sessions to students in their dormitories. A popular student service at some universities is a pre-examination review that students can watch in their own rooms. The professor conducting the review in a university production studio invites telephone calls from viewers who have questions and comments.

Other teachers are finding that videotaped explanations of concepts, processes, laboratory procedures, and so on help the student who has trouble mastering the material from textbook readings or classroom presentations alone. For one thing, a videotape can be played as often as a student desires, and the instructor on the tape never tires or loses patience. Some institutions even make special stipends available to encourage faculty members to undertake such projects for the improvement of teaching.

Instructional TV specialists and advocates have reason to be gratified in that their efforts are helping teachers attack problem areas in instruction. Yet, their sense of gratification is tempered by an awareness that a good number of the faculty involved in the survey referred to "made it clear that they value the instructional capacity of video and audio technologies, but the majority are more intensely focused on computers than either video or audio technologies."[10] Does this seeming endorsement portend that video will be largely supplanted as a way to supplement instruction once the flexible, effective computer software faculty appear to be yearning for is available? Rather, does it not mean that video designers and producers will be devoting their efforts more to making their materials interactive and staying attuned to the kinds of materials instructors need to address instructional problem areas?

EXTENDING INSTRUCTION EVEN MORE

The telecourse, the community college's most significant contribution to television-based distance teaching, has already been discussed. It has also been noted that 1 million or so Americans have enrolled in telecourses presented by PBS's Adult Learning Service alone since 1981. The newer technologies being referred to, cable television, satellite and microwave transmission, videocassettes, videodiscs, and slow-scan television, are now encouraging higher education institutions to reach still newer constituencies. The technologies and their applications in distance teaching keep proliferating. For example, channels of multi-channel cable TV systems can now be made "addressable," that is, so engineered that only viewers who subscribe to the special services receive them. This means more opportunities to extend instructional services to, say, special-interest professional/occupational groups too small to warrant the attention of open broadcasters.

What television has already wrought for the adult who must or who prefers to study at a distance is certainly remarkable. For a college to employ cable television to bring twenty-five adults a course in philosophy is a remarkable service, even though there are always the skeptics who will contend that the same twenty-five might very well enroll in an old-fashioned correspondence course. They question, in effect, the worth of the TV medium itself, and point to experience at the University of Mid-America where students who enrolled in an accounting telecourse ignored the TV programs and used only the printed study materials. They did as well in the final examination as those who had faithfully watched the programs.[11]

It could be that the accounting video programs were designed to divert and motivate as much as to instruct. Still, whether they were or not, television, as Walter Perry of the BOU argues, is an effective pacer of student progress and performs an important communitarian function. For many enrolled in conventional college classes, the classroom sessions are of most value in that they prod them to keep pace with the work assigned so as to profit from the professors' presentations and student discussions. So, too, the telecourse students are careful to complete required readings to derive maximum benefit from video programs. The programs also remind them that they are not alone as distant learners. Others are watching as well.

Then, too, to return to the twenty-five students enrolled in a philosophy telecourse, how many viewers with no interest in or need for college credit will also watch the programs? There are people who watch, and even read the prescribed texts, just because they are intellectually curious. Thus, the college under whose auspices the course is offered is performing a noteworthy public service. Indeed, many cable TV systems with active community-service channels allow colleges and universities time for cultural programs, features on health care, child care, and the like. Some colleges, particularly community colleges, schedule whole blocks of time on cable channels. Sadly, others take little or no advantage of the opportunity when proffered.

Noncredit Programming for the Curious Adult

The matter of programming for noncredit viewers is an opportunity and a challenge for any college, especially the public community college, which is chartered to serve all segments of its community. In fact, some community colleges now present programming on television that is designed to encourage adults who never finished high school to prepare for high school equivalency and general educational development (GED) examinations. A video course consisting of a series of programs and study materials has been available from the State of Kentucky's ETV authority for some years and has been widely used by institutions across the country. For that matter, The Learning Channel, a national satellite-based broadcast service of the Appalachian Community Service Network, now makes the series available on cable television around the country as part of its diversified schedule of adult education programs.

Community colleges are concerned with combatting the problem of functional illiteracy, which is being described on all sides as a major national issue. Four-year colleges and universities, one would also assume, have an opportunity and a responsibility in this area of public service, especially publicly supported institutions. As yet, only little has been done on television to relieve adult illiteracy, although a nationwide attack employing television and other media seems inevitable. Such an attack will require the cooperation of specialists to be found in the upper-division institutions as well as in the community colleges — linguists, anthropologists, psychologists, ethnologists, and others.

No one doubts the affective and motivational powers of television. These powers can best be brought into play in the interest of the public service. It is unlikely that men and women who lack basic reading, writing, and computational skills can learn them directly from TV programs, but the programs can make them acutely aware of their need for help and move them to take steps to do something about their disabling deficiencies. Further, television enables adult educators to reach them without creating embarrassment, since they can reach them in the privacy of their own homes.

Both the ABC Network and PBS for a time did air messages urging adults with literacy problems to seek assistance. In the 1970s, the BBC presented materials designed to encourage non-English speaking immigrants and others with literacy problems to seek help readily available in their communities. Community colleges involved in GED TV instruction are concerned not so much with employing the programs themselves for direct instruction as they are in encouraging viewers to come to their campuses for tutoring, face-to-face help, computer drill, and so forth.

Television — cable television, in particular — can be an important public service resource for higher education at all levels. Unfortunately, uses of television for informal adult education are not as extensive as educators had hoped. For one thing, like their brothers in open broadcast, cable TV operators are wary of tarnishing their public images by showing programs of subprofessional quality. On-campus lectures and symposia often do not convert readily into TV fare and have little appeal for viewers who are channel hopping. In short, instructional programs that hold the attention of general audiences are not in oversupply. As colleges have learned, it takes more time and resources than they are willing or able to invest to produce usable programs. A college soon discovers that it is not an easy task to fill a cable schedule for the four hours every week the cable operator has offered. The cable operator soon begins to complain of the lack of imagination in the programs the college submits, the redundancy of the programs, and so on.

"Software" Problems

Users and educators alike are plagued by the chronic shortage of programming. If only, the complaint is heard, the software could keep up with the hardware, or, as Thoreau remarked, Maine could find something to say to Texas. Given the present unpredictable patterns of support for instructional TV production in the United States, can we ever expect to see an inventory of college-level telecourses sufficient in scope to enable the distant learner to complete even a significant portion of degree-directed study via television? Will instructional TV practitioners ever coordinate their planning and activities so that we can avoid the expensive waste represented by the Annenberg/CPB Project funding a telecourse in introductory psychology at the same time a reputable and successful producer like Coastline Community College is also at work on one?

To date, the telecourses seen by distant learners on PBS stations, The Learning Channel, and local stations have come from a handful of community colleges, consortia of institutions organized for specific productions, several universities, a few state-supported public broadcast agencies, and, of course, in recent years, the Annenberg/CPB Project. Most major productions are cooperative efforts, as we have seen, with the institution making the largest investment in the effort reserving the right to market and distribute the products nationally.

No matter how supportive governmental and private organizations have been in the past, they are not reliable continuing sources of support, subject as they are to changes in their administration and policies. Somehow, if a sizable inventory of marketable television-based distance learning materials is ever to be maintained, stable ways of financing production from one year to the next must be devised. Some educators hoped that the Annenberg/CPB Project when first announced in 1979 would help solve the problem of making high-quality, degree-directed TV and audio courses accessible to distant learners on a continuous basis. Originally, it was thought that the Project might in its impact resemble the BOU, and even go beyond it by reaching "a broader audience, including adults not going after degrees." The "broad aim" of the project was "to support the production of high-quality, college-level courses through existing as well as developing telecommunications systems." However, as a skeptic might put it, the project betrayed its innocence of the American higher education culture, and hoped to be all things to all people. It would help the young and their parents get a foot up the higher education ladder at a time of soaring tuition costs; it would help older people undergoing the mid-career changes that mark our changing economy acquire new knowledge and skills; it would give the intelligent general viewer a taste of college-level instruction without having to take examinations and write term papers.[12] Its close alliance with the Corporation for Public Broadcasting (CPB), established by Congress as the funding mechanism for PBS, has not proved to be an unmixed blessing for the distant learner who has an eventual degree in mind or to the institution willing to accredit the distant learner's efforts. Too many products have seemed designed primarily to provide PBS stations with prime time programming for general audiences in a period of dwindling resources for public broadcasters. The programs are broadly educational, but their content often does not jibe with the course descriptions in many college catalogs, especially at the introductory undergraduate level.

In its 1989 *Proposal Guidelines,* the Project still professed its broad objectives, though in guarded terms: "The Annenberg/CPB Project was created in 1981 to enhance the quality and availability of higher education through the use of telecommunications and information technologies." More specifically, by spending $10 million a year for fifteen years, the Project planned "to develop course materials, tools and delivery systems that increase opportunities for those who wish to obtain a college-level education, especially at the baccalaureate level."[13]

Halfway through the planned duration of the Project, which, as indicated, has been suspended because of questions raised as to its tax exempt status, about twenty-five courses are available for use, with a half-dozen or so in some stage of development. The courses are leased or sold to users through a marketing and distribution agency selected by the Project. A number of so-called demonstration projects have also been funded. These are designed to test the instructional potential of the "tools" mentioned in the *Guidelines* cited above. Agencies and institutions have received awards to investigate a laser-based disc data base of materials as a way to create courses on ancient Greece, videodiscs for simulating laboratory experiments, computer conferences for supporting and linking distant learners, and electronic text for delivering study materials as well as full credit courses.

All in all, the Annenberg/CPB Project, while it was active, added courses and materials at an impressive rate to the existing inventory. The size and variety of the inventory itself are impressive, even when we allow for obsolescence, foreseeing an active life for most telecourses of about eight years without revisions. Yet neither from the standpoint of the public broadcaster nor from that of the distance educator has this collection proved an unalloyed boon. On one hand, handsome as the video programs are, not all the telecourses have the audience appeal a public broadcaster likes. For example, neither *The Write Course,* a course in English composition revolving around self-conscious attempts at a story line and human interest, nor *The Mechanical Universe,* a two-semester physics course that combines documentary approaches with a professor lecturing and demonstrating, holds appeal for audiences of the size PBS stations want at prime time. On the other hand, some of the courses challenge the ingenuity of eager institutional adopters, since they must struggle to make them conform to the requirements of college-credit curricula. Courses such as *War and Peace in the Nuclear Age* or *The Pacific World* are somewhat exotic in an undergraduate curriculum. They also disappoint others who hoped that the Annenberg/CPB Project might lead to the development of a demanding liberal arts degree program for adult learners. When the project discontinued operations, the outlook was for a disjointed medley of courses, with emphasis on business and business-oriented courses.

Annenberg/CPB telecourse producers also fell prey to an ill that besets instructional producers courting general audiences. They adopted approaches that excite suspicions of a lack of scholarly balance and disinterest. A good example of this is a telecourse entitled *The Africans,* which provoked fierce controversy when it was first shown on PBS and was attacked as propagandizing one point of view. One of the co-sponsors of the course, the National Endowment for the Humanities, even withdrew its name as a co-funder to protest what its officials alleged was a biased approach.

Perhaps some of the problems users have with the content of the courses stem from the method used to solicit proposals for projects. The proposals submitted pretty much determined what the overall telecourse curriculum was to be. That is, too much hinged on what the applicant thought would make a good course and good TV viewing, and not enough upon realizing a predetermined, though flexible, curricular framework. True, there are Project courses available that distant learners can apply without any difficulty to satisfy standard undergraduate requirements, but others, as indicated, fall into categories known as area studies (e.g., *China, Pacific World, Other America*) that have little relevance to most undergraduate curricula. In addition, thus far, the social sciences have been overrepresented. It is heartening to see that more attention was being given to the hard sciences and mathematics, which, of course, are resistant to entertaining presentation for broad audiences.

At present, there are in the collection a half-dozen video and three audio courses (these involving only a slight investment as compared to the costs of TV production) in science and mathematics.

The open solicitation of course proposals, the review of proposals by peer panels, and the understanding that courses should appeal to broad audiences also seem to have encouraged a certain trendiness in course selection. This reflects, it is true, the curriculum trendiness found on many American campuses. In any event, there are courses in nutrition, the state of the environment, and the history of women.

Probably the planners of the Project had in mind making available on television for all who tune in not only a university-level learning experience, but also a sample of the learning experiences now available to those lucky enough to attend the nation's elite institutions. Whether this is so or not, a good proportion of the awards made went to the more prestigious institutions and to individuals connected with prestigious organizations. This predisposition, unfortunately, does not always guarantee the best and most usable product for a distant learner who wants to complete basic undergraduate requirements on television. But there were signs before the suspension of activities that Annenberg/CPB officials were changing some of the early directions. As mentioned earlier, the Instructional Telecommunications Consortium, an affiliated agency of the American Association of Community and Junior Colleges, is interested in acquiring materials needed by its members. It negotiated with the Project for the production of five telecourses identified after a national survey of student needs: College Algebra, Child Development, Geology, Introduction to Philosophy, and Introduction to Literature. The Project awarded $3.2 million to support two of the courses, geology and literature. It should be noted that these courses are to be produced at lower cost than other Annenberg courses and that, according to the Southern California Consortium, the agent serving as the production manager, over 350 colleges are involved in prepurchasing the courses, which one can interpret as a sure sign that there is demand for the courses.

It is to the credit of Annenberg/CPB Project officials that they remained responsive to the misgivings expressed about the directions taken thus far. It should also be noted that, straddling as it does the worlds of public broadcast and higher education, it has had to move tentatively and without a sure sense of mission. Public broadcasters, on the whole, take their educational mission to be providing an intellectually respectable alternative to what is on the commercial channels. They do not regard themselves as formal arms of the educational systems.

The American higher education system is a fragmented one, with each institution and state authority carefully guarding its own autonomy. National "open universities" or "universities of the air" are alien to our system. It is unrealistic, therefore, to expect any project, no matter how well-funded, to develop a distinctive curriculum leading to a generalist bachelor's degree that colleges and universities will accept *in toto*. Within the last several years, however, there were unmistakable signs, as has already been indicated, that the Project was striving for a balance between courses with wide audience appeal, but resistant to incorporation into the credit curriculum, and narrower-interest courses that attract viewers seeking college credits. For example, the Project resurrected a practice of *Continental Classroom,* which was described earlier, by producing a course in *Western Civilization,* a staple in undergraduate curricula, revolving around the lectures of a well-known historian and dynamic teacher on the West Coast.

These changes are signaled by the Instructional Telecommunications Consortium's telecourse development project mentioned above, which will give prepurchasers a chance to participate in the determination of course content and the evaluation of pilot materials. This kind of cooperative planning and prepurchase arrangement, following user–needs assessment, has been carried out with great success for some years at the elementary and secondary levels by National Instructional Television (NIT) of Bloomington, Indiana. Periodically, after consultation with state and Canadian provincial education officers, NIT determines the common instructional TV needs of the schools. Once a common need is identified, NIT invites the states and provinces to purchase the materials in advance of actual production. The fees, proportioned to the purchaser's student population, underwrite development and studio production costs.

The Annenberg/CPB Project is a landmark and its products are reinvigorating distance higher education in this country by giving it greater visibility and by involving more colleges and universities, including some of the nation's leading institutions, in the preparation of distance teaching materials. These products have built a valuable inventory of materials for distance teaching and learning.

One can only conjecture as to what the shift in emphasis suggested by the award to the Instructional Telecommunications Consortium bodes for the future of the Project, should it resume operations and have a future. In a 1989 speech to members of the Instructional Telecommunications Consortium, the Project director, Mara Mayor, stated that "our first concern . . . has been with the student who cannot easily or regularly attend classes on campus — the distant learner."[14] If there is a future, one infers it might see a two-tiered kind of telecourse development, one made up of the more costly series that appeal to the broader TV audience, and the other, professor-centered and appealing primarily to credit student audiences. In fact, early in 1990 the Project announced a special funding initiative to encourage colleges, universities, and associations of the same to employ whatever information and telecommunications technologies are available to them to extend courses and academic services of all kinds to students who cannot come to campuses regularly. Presumably, some colleges will take advantage of the awards, ranging from $150,000 to $300,000 to bring high-enrollment, degree-directed courses originating in classrooms and lecture halls to students watching cable television and videocassettes off campus, and using the telephone, weekend sessions on campus, personal computers, and even fax machines for interaction with professors. All this would seem a sensible way of honoring the Project's broad original commitments and deriving more usable products from funds available.

Certainly the Annenberg/CPB Project inventory will not solve the problems of institutions that want to make really extensive uses of television-based materials. The Project, however, despite its uncertain status, has already performed a valuable function in supplying materials that can be used in a variety of ways both on and off campus. It also underwrote demonstrations of instructional applications of newer telecommunications technologies now on the market, the results of which will prove useful to institutions thinking of investing in such media. Finally, as already indicated, the Project's having endowed television- and telecommunications-based teaching with greater academic respectability is of tremendous assistance to proponents of media-based instruction and learning.

REACHING AUDIENCES WITH
SPECIALIZED NEEDS

If open-air broadcast were the only delivery means available to educators employing television, what chance would they have of reaching distant learners whose needs are narrower than those in pursuit of eventual bachelor's degrees? In fact, there is a diminishing demand for the traditional liberal arts education of the kind colleges have been offering since colonial times. Many colleges and universities now find their curricula in business, management, and computer science oversubscribed, whereas they are hard pressed to fill classes in the humanities and natural sciences. Telecourse enrollment data show that the preferences of these distance learners mirror those of conventional students. The three-year study of telecourse students and enrollments now being conducted by the Instructional Telecommunications Consortium discloses that basic courses in business and social science, especially psychology, are the most popular choices. A telecourse entitled *The Business of Management* is used by about half of the nearly 200 institutions represented in the survey, though we must keep in mind that most of the institutions involved are community colleges and many community college students occupy a sort of limbo since they are attending conventionally taught classes at the same time they are in telecourses.[15] No matter what shifts in curriculum preference take place on college campuses, we must anticipate that more and more adult distant learners will be looking for career and occupational training and opportunities, as life expectancy rises and mid-life career changes become more common.

As we have seen, distance educators need inexpensive ways of delivering instructional materials to groups with specialized interests. Cable television now goes into about 50 percent of American homes and steadily increases its penetration. Surveys of telecourse students and their viewing habits show that as many as 75 to 80 percent have VCRs in their homes (which also discloses something about the socioeconomic status of telecourse students). We have already discussed how so-called narrowcast transmission — microwave, for example — is serving distance learners on worksites and other locations.

The real virtue of these new video technologies is that they are ideally suited to narrow audiences, for example, engineers looking for advanced training; lawyers who want, or are required by laws of their states, to complete continuing professional education; and health professionals also required by law to stay abreast of latest developments in their fields. More recent cable systems are multi-channel, leaving free a number of channels for special purposes. Cable systems can replay programs at hours of the day and evening that fit even into the schedules of people who work at odd hours. The videocassette means even greater convenience for the busy adult. He or she can play programs as often as needed and whenever convenient.

The linkages and networking now possible are a real boon to the dedicated distance educator. A course, say, in mathematics can be recorded on videocassette from satellite transmission. Think of the ways the recorded videocassette can be copied and distributed. It can be fed into cable television and delivered to homes and community sites; sent via an ITFS system to schools and work sites; even delivered by hand — "bicycled" as the expression goes — to offices, industrial sites, and so forth.

The National Technological University

One flourishing distance teaching agency made possible by the new technologies is the already mentioned National Technological University (NTU), headquartered in Fort Collins, Colorado. NTU evolved from a service originally supplied by Colorado State University to local corporate clients. Videotapes and videocassettes of advanced engineering classes were "bicycled" out to corporate sites where qualified employees watched them and enrolled in the university for graduate credit. Nowadays, as already indicated, the classes are transmitted by satellite to locations all over the country.

Although NTU is an association of some twenty-eight engineering schools, including some of the nation's most prominent, it itself is chartered as a private, nonprofit, degree-granting institution. It awards master of science degrees in several fields, and draws its faculty from member colleges and universities. The member college faculties determine what courses are to be completed by students to fulfill degree requirements. Courses originate from the classrooms of member institutions and are sent directly via satellite to corporate and other sites, where they are viewed by working engineers, scientists, and technical managers. To enroll in NTU courses, a professional must be employed by a company that sponsors the programs on its site. With some exceptions, uniform tuition fees apply to all courses listed in the NTU catalog. Textbooks and supporting study materials are also prescribed for courses.

Provision is made for two-way communication, so that instruction is interactive. Students are free to reach teachers by telephone if they view classes as they are being taught in the classroom. Otherwise they can get in touch with professors via PC, electronic mail, and audio teleconferences. Faculty can also be reached on their office telephones at scheduled hours.

NTU also broadcasts live short courses and seminars in special topics to keep engineers and technologists abreast of developments in rapidly changing fields. All the affiliated colleges and universities have satellite uplinks on their campuses, which means that all are capable of adding live courses to the network.

One other feature of the NTU operation deserves notice, that is, its willingness to tailor programs directly to a company's particular training needs. A single company, for a special fee, can receive special noncredit programs for its own employees.

NTU, it should be noted, is not the only agency providing television-based services of this kind, though it is the most ambitious, since it is national in scope. The engineering college of Stanford University has been offering a similar program for some years in California's Bay Area. Other institutions — the Massachusetts Institute of Technology comes immediately to mind — also utilize video to extend professional development services. At this point, further mention should be made of the exciting and perhaps seminal Star Schools Project, a demonstration supported by the U.S. Department of Education. The project delivers via satellite television live interactive video and computer-based instruction to rural schools, as well as college-level courses in mathematics and science to high school students capable of working at advanced levels. The purpose of the project is to equalize educational opportunities for students in schools unable to provide full services. The following agencies are participating in the demonstration phase: the Midlands Consortium, located at Oklahoma State University; the TI-IN Network of San Antonio, Texas; the Technical Education Resource Center of Cambridge, Massachusetts; and the Satellite Educational Resources Consortium of Columbia, South Carolina. If successful, this project may very well make distance teaching an integral part of public education from elementary school to the college and university.

Satellite technology is enabling professional organizations of all kinds to present continuing education programs wherever there are satellite downlinks to receive them. Downlinks, fortunately for those interested in using TV technology for continuing professional development, become less expensive all the time.

Narrowcast Services

On several occasions in preceding pages, note has been taken of the instructional uses of "narrowcast," as opposed to open broadcast, for distance teaching. Colleges and universities and associations of institutions throughout the country now employ Instructional Television

Fixed Service (ITFS), a low-power, point-to-point transmission, to send instruction out from classrooms to satellite locations and work sites. Although special receiving antennae and signal converters are needed to receive and play the programs on regular TV sets, ITFS is economically feasible for most institutions, since the start-up and operational costs are modest.

As mentioned earlier, in response to pressures brought to bear by educational and public service groups, the FCC reserved a band of special ITFS frequencies for educational and public agencies some years ago, with the channels licensed to users in clusters of four. Unfortunately, in some areas of the country, channels were left unapplied for, and in a later action the FCC awarded some of the unused channels to commercial users and permitted some educational licensees to share channel time with commercial interests.

Impressive as the distribution potential of video media like ITFS and cable television are alone, they are even greater and more flexible when combined with other technologies. For example, cable and ITFS channels now receive and retransmit signals from satellites. Thus, NTU and PBS Adult Learning Service programs can be sent via satellite and delivered to local audiences in a variety of ways — through ITFS, cable, or videocassettes. The satellite, in effect, has become a storehouse of instructional materials for higher education users.

One midwestern community college, Kirkwood of Cedar Rapids, Iowa, is invariably singled out as a model of an institution of modest size and resources utilizing the narrowcast technologies imaginatively and successfully. The college's service area spreads out over a seven-county area, which includes several large communities as well as a number of rural communities. Commuting distances for residents living on the outer edges of the service area are formidable. Kirkwood is exemplary in that narrowcast technologies permit it to provide comprehensive community college programs over a large area. What is noteworthy is that the programs can be provided at a cost a relatively small two-year college can afford.

The college could certainly never have borne the costs — or the risks, in view of demographic uncertainties — of building satellite or secondary campuses. Instead, to equalize educational opportunities for all its constituents, it chose to build an interactive telecommunications system, which includes microwave transmission and reception facilities; four ITFS channels on the main campus, plus additional ones at other sites; and two cable TV channels. The college also owns a satellite downlink, which it uses to bring video teleconferences originating all over the country to groups in the community, as well as telecourses and other educational programs.

Microlinks connect off-campus classrooms located in high schools to the main college campus. Video and audio signals pass in two directions along these microwave connections. Thus, a student sitting in a classroom some twenty miles away from the main campus is not a mere observer. He or she talks to the instructor and fellow students on the main campus by audio connection. Although classes most often originate on the main campus, some off-campus classrooms used for remote teaching are equipped with video, so that a teacher can originate a class away from the main campus every now and then.

Kirkwood students also can view a full range of college-sponsored programs in their homes and in community locations. The programming includes prerecorded telecourses; special programs coming from the main campus and remote sites; films and videotapes from outside sources; programs about college activities and special services; and programs featuring faculty and student talent.[16]

Networking technology to overcome constraints on instructional services imposed by distance and uneven distribution of population is part of the strategy of four-year colleges as well, though one would expect the community colleges to be more heavily involved by virtue of their strong commitment to reach all kinds of constituencies. California State University at Chico in Northern California has a service area much larger than that of Kirkwood Community College, some 33,000 square miles, in fact, or 20 percent of the total area of the state, with some 600,000 residents dispersed throughout towns and rural areas. In the early 1980s, the university's continuing education division linked thirteen regional learning centers by microwave/ITFS systems, the most distant almost 175 miles from the main campus in Chico. So-called "translators," devices that strengthen signals and send them over and around mountains and other obstacles, are utilized to extend the range of the microwave/ITFS transmission.

At present, about 600 students are enrolled in CSU/Chico centers in some 25 courses. The extension service, in fact, is no longer regional. In 1984, the university installed a satellite uplink on campus, and its TV courses are now being delivered across North America. The Chico system allows for two-way audio traffic, so that students can question instructors when courses are coming directly from classrooms. Regional community college and high school classrooms where distant learners view video courses are stocked with library and other materials needed.

As a former teachers' college, Chico has a strong teacher-training program and enrolls many prospective and in-service teachers in telecommunications-based education courses. It also offers degree-directed computer science courses on ITFS. Out-of-state students employed by corporations participating in the Chico satellite-delivered service are also enrolled in courses leading to the bachelor's degree in computer science. Telecourses are also offered to advanced-level high school students in rural areas.[17]

Both Kirkwood and California State University at Chico are examples of how the judicious employment of the newer video technologies can enrich and diversify extension services. Both institutions share problems stemming from citizens who are denied easy access to campuses because of distance. Video technologies are solving these problems at modest cost. It cannot be emphasized too much that in both institutions top-level administrators are firmly committed to uses of technology.

Instances of imaginative deployment of video technologies for the purpose of equalizing higher education opportunities could be multiplied. The examples described here were chosen not because they are the best that might be found, but because they demonstrate how distance teaching problems can be solved. Actually, a broad range of technology-based distance teaching and learning approaches is now available, and a broad range of institutions offers the programs. Educators and others interested in telecommunications-based distance teaching are again referred to Raymond Lewis's useful survey in his 1983 *Meeting Learners' Needs Through Telecommunications*. One can only hope that this compendium will be updated regularly or that new surveys will be undertaken periodically.

Evaluating the Effort

In preceding chapters, evaluations made of television-based instruction have been alluded to on a number of occasions. For the most part, however, these were references to attitudinal assessments, that is, to studies made of the feelings of students and faculty members about TV instruction. Some readers are undoubtedly wondering what kinds of investigations have been done to determine how well students do in their telecourses and how much they learn from them. Other questions also arise about the students themselves. What are they like? For what kinds of people can we predict success in TV courses? What do students like in their courses? What do they dislike?

Still other readers may wonder how thoroughly telecourse design, about which we have said a good deal, has been evaluated. Others may wonder what changes, if any, have been made in telecourse procedures and design on the basis of investigations conducted.

Specialists in educational evaluation, as is well known, often speak an impenetrable language, or so it seems to the innocent nonspecialist. What follows in this chapter is not intended for the specialist. It does not pretend to be anything more than a brief summary, in plain language, of research a general reader is likely to find of interest.

With distance education emerging as a matter of major concern, a body of research is growing around the world. For the English-speaking community, a good deal of information has come out of the British Open University's (BOU) Distance Education Research Group, which has sponsored monographs on selected distance teaching systems, as well as on teaching strategies and student support services. The recently established *U.S. Journal of Distance Education,* recipient of an Annenberg/CPB Project grant and headquartered at Pennsylvania State University, promises to become another useful source. Foreign journals — the *Canadian Journal of Distance Education,* Australia's *Distance Education,* the London-based *Epistolodidaktika,* and the BOU's *Teaching at a Distance* (now unfortunately discontinued) — have published studies of media teaching functions, media utilization, and support services for distance learners. During its brief and controversial lifetime, the University of Mid-America (UMA) sponsored studies of instructional materials marketing, student needs assessment, and the factors determining whether or not an adult enrolls in a distance learning project. Other UMA researchers focused on evaluating the design of distance teaching materials, with a view to revising and improving those already in use. Their efforts were influenced and guided to a large extent by investigators at the BOU.

Studies of telecourse uses, of student performance in telecourses, and of telecourse student characteristics have appeared in this country since the 1950s. In 1967, the U.S. Office of Education underwrote a summary of the research in film and television conducted up to that time, a publication, even though now over thirty years old, that is still useful. The findings reported therein about how well and how much students learn by television have been confirmed and reconfirmed in subsequent studies. Before looking at any of the investigations, however, we should note that research efforts in this country, with respect to telecourses in particular, have sometimes been driven more by the desire to promote than to assess in a disinterested fashion. As the author of an already cited survey of telecourses remarked, "Unfortunately, systematic attempts to evaluate telecourses have been the exception rather than the rule."[1]

STUDENT PERFORMANCE IN TELECOURSES

Not surprisingly, the first question asked about teaching via television is, can students learn as much as they do in conventional classes? What, precisely, "as much" means is quite another question.

During the 1960s and 1970s, investigators were tireless in their comparisons of TV student performance with that of students taking classroom courses in the same subjects.[2] Results of most studies conducted under controlled conditions concurred that there were no significant differences in the performances. Indeed, in the period when the performance comparisons were done frequently, the finding of "no significant difference" became an inside joke among instructional TV practitioners.

Among the earliest of the carefully controlled studies was one conducted by Chicago's TV College. Chicago investigators, before arriving at their conclusions, were careful to compare TV students and on-campus community college students of comparable age and educational background. This meant, in effect, that they matched adult telecourse students working on their own at home with adult part-time students enrolled in the same courses on City Colleges of Chicago campuses. Course content was equivalent, and common testing materials were used. The Chicago studies showed that the TV students, who typically were highly motivated adults, tended to outperform their on-campus counterparts. They also made clear that unselected community college students of normal college age permitted to take TV courses in the classroom did not perform satisfactorily unless they were provided follow-up discussion regularly by live classroom teachers.

Investigations of BOU student performance corroborate these findings in general. Students admitted to the BOU who would not have qualified for admission to a conventional university do less well than those who do. Former Vice Chancellor Walter Perry has an interesting explanation for the slightly better performance of the first group of students admitted in 1971, an explanation that only confirms the importance of maturity in distance learners. He accounts for the seeming anomaly on the ground that the then median entry age was 27 and that, therefore, the first group to be admitted was not really a representative one. The relatively high median age is an indication that there was present an unusually high level of motivation.[3] Once aware of these findings, readers can appreciate why academically disadvantaged adults and immature students are handicapped in distance learning projects and, consequently, enroll in small numbers. This reality causes discomfort for some adult educators. Ironically, part of the rationale for open and distance learning projects is to equalize opportunities for the disadvantaged. However, experience provides abundant evidence that adults in need of remedial-level instruction who enroll in college telecourses usually lack the self-discipline required for success in independent study and become discouraged quickly.

Although TV teaching is not for everyone, it is indisputable that mature, motivated adults can learn as well via television as they can in conventionally taught classes. However, reservations and qualifications must be added. One prominent college-level instructional TV researcher, Leslie Purdy, sums up the issue well: "When used as a part of a system composed of print materials, study and evaluation devices, and other instructional services, broadcast television is highly effective instruction."[4] In short, we can assert that a motivated learner who watches instructional video programs instead of attending regular classroom sessions, reads the textbooks and other materials prescribed, completes written assignments, and follows the course study guide faithfully can be expected to perform as well as a conventionally taught student of similar maturity and background. We must always keep in mind, however, that, whenever we speak of performance, we mean performance as measured by the standard measures of academic achievement, that is, by examinations, written projects, and so on. As every college student knows, classroom courses, especially well-taught ones, have dimensions that defy assessment by end-of-term examinations. For example, besides having mastered a certain amount of content or a set of skills, students often leave a class with their attitudes toward the subject matter and its value changed. The same thing, of course, can be said to some degree of a well-designed and well-supported telecourse. Measuring simply how much factual knowledge a student has taken away tells us very little about total effect.

In the long run, what counts most is what merchandisers call customer satisfaction. What is really encouraging to proponents of teaching by television is that surveys disclose a high level of student satisfaction. Chicago's TV College, which enabled 400 or so adults to complete a full two-year college program on television and thousands more to complete sizable portions of the program, once distributed a questionnaire to former students who had moved on to conventional four-year colleges and universities to gather information as to how they rated their experiences learning by television. Gratifyingly, most of the 300 respondents stated that they found that they could learn as much by television as they did in the conventional classroom. They also indicated — even more to the gratification of the questionnaire distributors — that their performance in conventional classes at the four-year colleges and universities to which they had transferred their television-earned credits was about the same as it had been in their TV courses. There was no falling off, as some had predicted there would be, when they moved on to advanced-level conventional courses. In addition, ". . . they all judged their television courses to be better organized and more effectively presented than the conventionally taught courses . . . in the colleges to which they had transferred."[5]

Despite the testimonials of students themselves and the evidence that students can learn by television, doubts still linger in some academic circles as to the effectiveness of telecourses. Some of these center around the value of the video components. The compilers of a 1986 report evaluating the student outcomes of televised instruction commissioned by the Annenberg/CPB Project state unequivocally that "the educational value of telecourses remains in dispute." They go on to assert that telecourses do not offer any "educational advantages over traditional media for the same population of students." By "traditional media," one presumes they mean the conventional instructional methods. A lack of "educational advantage" means, one infers, that telecourses by virtue of their being courses that employ media possess no intrinsic instructional superiority. To put the matter another way, the authors of the report are asking if the electronic media as such — video and audio — make any difference in teaching and learning effectiveness.

The authors discuss the presentations of two Annenberg/CPB Project–supported telecourses, *The Constitution: That Delicate Balance,* usable as a credit course in political science, and *The New Literacy,* an introduction to computer science. They compare how the courses were offered at several sites and seem to conclude that there is no way to evaluate how much gain there was in student learning as a result of various components built into the telecourses. They attribute differences in learning to variations in the student support from site to site. One support instructor demanded more reading from his telecourse students than did others, just as some conventional instructors do. Another instructor demanded very little reading. At one site, the students attended more follow-up classroom sessions than at another. One support instructor was sullen about his involvement in the telecourse, whereas another was enthusiastic.[6]

All of this, of course, tells us little about the function or the effectiveness of the video elements in a telecourse, but it does tell us something that adopters of telecourses soon learn: the user institution can add an important dimension to the learner's experience. As noted earlier, studies of student performance focus on test scores and grades on assignments. They are seldom, if ever, useful in determining what the video component in itself adds to the efficacy of instruction. Perhaps all we can conclude safely is that video programs can, as Walter Perry contends, pace the student's progress, and give him or her a sense of being part of something. If they are well-produced, they can, of course, make taking a course a more pleasurable experience, mixing instruction with delight. In short, television-based and face-to-face instruction are certainly not the same as educational experiences, but they can be of equal value when it comes to student achievement as this is conventionally measured.

Yet the question as to what the TV medium contributes is far from irrelevant. A common reaction of skeptical faculty members when shown a well-produced video sequence is to ask if it is worth all the trouble and expense, especially when a live teacher can tell students very quickly what the point is. Such an objection may seem Philistine and show insensitivity to the affective and motivational power of television. It is usually futile to try to counter it by pointing out that television has its own language and its own rhetoric, or to argue that its potential is wasted when it is used solely to show talking faces telling viewers what the point is.

An instructional TV researcher reiterates what others have said when she concludes that it "has been established, unequivocally and irrevocably, that a well-designed and produced television program can and does teach." She goes on to remind us, however, that studies comparing TV and conventional teaching that begin with the question, "Does it teach better than . . . ?" are generally uninformative and inappropriate.[7] As she says, the wrong question is being asked. Perhaps we should ask if the means employed are disproportionate to the end. Television can be an expensive medium to employ to teach distance learners English composition. Is an expenditure of several million dollars justifiable when the instructional goal, to teach students to write simple expository prose, can be achieved as well with much less fanfare? It is extremely unlikely that such a course can be clothed in delight for large PBS audiences.

Considerable investigation has been devoted to determining "what media attributes are valuable in specific learning circumstances." Psychologists and TV specialists have investigated the instructional values of visual images, color, and combinations of audio and video. The research to date, as one multi-media specialist concludes, is inconclusive: ". . . there is no single identifiable attribute or variable inherent in these instructional media which can account for more learning across time than any other."[8] Even where television-based instruction flourishes, that is, in the community colleges and community college consortia, one cannot conclude that the TV medium itself is a key element in the achievement of the learner involved. It is always disturbing for instructional TV proponents to discover that some telecourse students do well without even watching video programs, or watching them only infrequently. The textbook and study guide are enough for them, just as the textbook is enough for students who can perform at a satisfactory level in conventional instruction without attending classes regularly. In some instances, another electronic medium — the computer or the audio cassette — could be used just as effectively and at lower cost. In short, seemingly successful employments, as well as unsuccessful employments, of television must always be assessed within the context of student levels of motivation, maturity, and prior academic preparation.

Despite its shortcomings and expense, television remains the favorite medium in media-based instruction, although within purely academic environments, that is, within institutions, it may be displaced in large part by the personal computer. Yet, like film, but without all the trouble and fuss for teachers, it brings the real world into the classroom and enriches instruction beyond measure. Nowadays, university students of international relations or of Russian or Chinese language and culture can watch videotapes of Soviet or Chinese announcers reading their versions of world news. This marvel is made possible by the satellite and the videotape recorder. In *Understanding Media,* Marshall McLuhan, the oracle of the electronic age, wrote:

> It [television] has created a taste for all experience in depth that affects language teaching as much as car styles. Since TV, nobody is happy with book knowledge of French or English poetry. The unanimous cry is, "Let's talk French," and "Let the bard be heard."

Readers who have seen the Annenberg/CPB Project's *French in Action,* the BBC's *The Shakespeare Plays,* or BBC language series in French, Italian, Spanish, Russian, and Modern Greek know that TV producers have really taken this pronouncement to heart.

No matter that we cannot confidently tick off the properties of the TV medium that improve or expedite learning achievement, the fact remains that the medium when well employed captures a student's attention with its rich multi-sensory impact. This impact can be particularly significant, obviously, with subject matter that demands visual experience, the kind of visual experience that television can supply so well. Even though some American viewers of the Annenberg/CPB *Art of the Western World* may be distracted and even annoyed by a long-haired, Levis-clad host, speaking with an exaggerated Oxbridge drawl, they are still entranced when a TV camera moves around a piece of sculpture, lingering on details that most museum-goers miss.

STUDENT ATTRITION

Attrition, or dropout, is a sensitive issue with all educators, and particularly with distance educators. As is well known, high dropout rate has always plagued nonproprietary correspondence instruction. Some readers may remember the United States Armed Forces Institute (USAFI), which supplied so many correspondence college and university courses for servicemen during World War II and the years immediately following. It was eventually dissolved when Congress cut off its funding because of the high dropout rate.

Experienced instructional TV practitioners have learned ways to reduce attrition in telecourses. They discourage students whose deficient academic backgrounds make them poor risks for independent study programs. It has also been noted that eighteen- and nineteen-year-old students in community colleges are unpromising candidates for telecourses, unless they are provided regular face-to-face and supplemental instruction and support. Community colleges, as well as colleges and universities that offer telecourses term after term, schedule a variety of supportive services for students, including required orientation sessions at the start of a term, face-to-face sessions on campus with support instructors, telephone conferences each week, telephone "hot lines," and so forth. To help them gauge their progress throughout the course, the distant learners are armed with banks of self-scoring tests and quizzes. Some institutions with strong commitment to the electronic technologies try to keep distant learners more actively involved in their courses by using the computer to correct quizzes and recommending corrective action if such is indicated.

Another method of attacking the problem of dropout is by making telecourses as interactive as possible. One-way video of the kind presented by the PBS Adult Learning Service on open broadcast can discourage the student with deficient study skills. For this reason, military and industrial trainers prefer methods that combine video and computer technologies, so that trainees are required to respond actively and display a degree of mastery of what has been taught in one unit before they can go on to a next. It is only reasonable to assume that the greater a learner's chances of success, the more unlikely he or she is to withdraw from a course.

Some adult educators, in fact, have been trying to single out the conditions needed to give a distant learner the maximum chance of success. One comments that the "distance" in Distance Education theory is to be reckoned not by how many miles students are separated from their instructors, but by "the extent to which a particular teaching–learning relationship was individual and dialogic."[9] What this means in plainer language is that the distance educator must match the instructional medium to be employed to a student's level of ability and consequent need for interaction or dialogue. Computer-assisted instruction allowing for give-and-take between student and instructor can individualize teaching for those who need continuous support. Face-to-face or telephone conferences can supply dialogue for those who need occasional instructor support.

There are some factors in attrition, of course, over which distance teaching institutions have little or no control. Students often drop out for reasons other than discouragement, lack of progress, or dissatisfaction with the course presentation. Like their counterparts in conventional classrooms, they withdraw because of illness, changes in work schedules, or problems at home. Yet, there are obvious steps an institution can take to prevent a certain proportion of the attrition it may be experiencing. Some would-be enrollees should be urged to take remedial-level or preparatory courses. When the Chicago TV College started in 1956, there were adults who hastened to enroll in its courses in a naive belief that these might be easy ways to earn college credits. It was obvious that such candidates had to be discouraged. As was stated earlier, the BOU advises applicants clearly unprepared for university-level study to take preparatory courses. These procedures, of course, entail the extra expense of supplying counseling services for distant learners, or at least making sure that they have the prerequisites for whatever courses presuppose prior courses.

Outside the United States, concern over student attrition in distance teaching institutions has prompted lively interest in finding ways to help distant learners learn. Such concern becomes especially intense when a governmental agency supporting a distance learning university expresses its dismay at the low total of graduates. For example, only about one in five of the BOU's students ever completes a degree. This, of course, does not mean that the other four are dropouts. Many simply take as many courses as they feel they need. Nonetheless, government officials, looking at the gross product, are unimpressed by these explanations. BOU officials look for ways to minimize dropout. As was mentioned earlier, the BOU has adopted a shrewd policy of trial registration, allowing students to defer official enrollment until a certain point in the term. Nor do they have to pay their fees in full until this trial period has ended. One wonders why U.S. colleges and universities offering telecourses do not adopt a version of this policy, especially those whose tuition fees are higher than those of the public community colleges in their areas offering telecourses.

Canada's Athabasca University, an open-learning institution that employs TV technologies among other media in its distance teaching system, undertook a study in 1980 to determine why its attrition rate was so high. One purpose of the study was to discover instructional approaches and services that might encourage more students to finish their courses. They were following the example of the BOU, which had commissioned the BBC to produce a TV series to help adults learn how to learn. British Columbia's Knowledge Network, an association of institutions offering both secondary and degree-directed postsecondary instruction, has also developed similar materials.[10]

IMPROVING STUDENT RETENTION

Any college offering distant learners formal instruction, whether television-based or mediated by some other means, should be able to retain 60 to 70 percent of its students, if it maintains an adequate student support system. The BOU is able to achieve its enviable retention (or "success") rate through its more than 250 fully staffed study centers located in the United Kingdom. The staff members include a complement of tutor–counselors who work face to face with students coming to the centers. The centers themselves contain computer terminals for student use, film equipment, videocassette and audio-cassette players, and TV receivers. According to most observers, the BOU owes its success to its combining a multi-media teaching package with individualized tutorial functions carried on in accessible locations.

In this country, regular and successful users of telecourses keep a sharp eye fixed on attrition rates, and are always trying to discover why distant learners do not complete their courses. Dallas Community College District, a leading producer and user of telecourses, regularly checks on the causes of dropout by calling and interviewing on the telephone students who withdraw. Dallas administrators also request reports on dropouts from telecourse support instructors who are in frequent contact with distant students. Instructors concur that withdrawal from a course seldom stems from dissatisfaction with the course itself. As stated earlier, job, family, and other personal problems are usually the precipitating factors. In addition, the Dallas studies confirm the Chicago TV College surveys done at an earlier date: some students do not find telecourses the "easy" credit they anticipated.

Some investigators have tried to devise ways to identify in advance factors that predict success or failure for telecourse students. The formulas, it turns out not surprisingly, are reflections of student socioeconomic profiles. They also are based on signs of reliability and self-discipline. Thus, students whose postal zip codes suggest that they suffer socioeconomic disadvantage are generally poor risks for independent study. A student who fails to complete and return an informational questionnaire distributed with course study materials is likely to be unreliable and lacking in self-discipline. The same can be said of students who do not attend the orientation sessions designed to acquaint them with course requirements. Common sense indicates that such signs of irresponsibility are predictors of failure.[11]

One reason colleges and universities employing telecommunications media to reach distant learners join associations and consortia is to apply the experiences of others in improving student retention. As for retention in the telecourse, it should be remembered that its very design presupposes active supportive instruction and thus encourages a student to persist. The more effective the support — particularly any support that encourages student interaction with both learning materials and the support instructor — the less the likelihood of student withdrawal. Still, as by now is obvious to the reader, the successful telecourse students must be self-motivated.

TELECOURSE STUDENTS' CHARACTERISTICS

Educators who design distance learning programs are often driven also by a desire to make education open to all — the disadvantaged, adults who were deprived of opportunities in their youth, as well as adults who wasted early chances and yearn for a second chance. From the standpoint of those who nurse egalitarian dreams, enrollments in open and distant learning projects — in the BOU or in U.S. community college telecourses — give scant reason for hope that a goodly number of citizens at whom the projects are aimed are responding. Surveys of men and women who enroll in telecourses show little or no evidence that these noble egalitarian goals are being realized. For example, the Telecourse Student Survey being conducted currently by the Instructional Telecommunications Consortium only confirms what most instructional TV practitioners already knew, that is, that two-thirds of those who enroll in telecourses enroll in conventional classes on campuses at the same time. It must be emphasized, however, that most respondents are from community colleges. Even with this qualification, nonetheless, we are safe in concluding that television is not an alternative for these people. Rather, it affords them a way to take more courses without increasing their travel time to and from a campus.

Readers must also bear in mind that figures to be reported in this section are derived from surveys of community college students enrolled in lower-division, undergraduate courses. They do not, therefore, reflect the characteristics, demographic or otherwise, of the increasing numbers of men and women who are enrolling in television-based, advanced-level instruction in specialized areas — the engineers, the business professionals, the health sciences professionals. We also must make allowances for demographic variations from one region to another. National samples of telecourse students, for example, may show 8 to 10 percent of telecourse students to be Black, whereas in Northern Illinois, for example, with its concentration of Black population, there may be as many as 20 percent. Likewise, a national sample may show Hispanic students representing only 5 or 6 percent, whereas a survey conducted at Miami-Dade Community College will show a decidedly higher figure.

Sex

In the United States, a majority of telecourse students are female, ranging from 60 percent to as high as 75 percent in some places. It is tempting to conjecture as to the reasons for this. One, no doubt, is that many American women are intent on building careers outside the home. Courses on television are a chance to make a start without having to leave home and neglecting responsibilities. Another is that women, as a group, seem to possess the degree of responsibility we have noted as being prerequisite to success in independent study.

The proportion of women enrolled in the BOU, as we have seen, is markedly lower. There they have been consistently underrepresented. This difference must be attributed to dissimilar outlooks and expectations in the United States and the United Kingdom.

Age

Most telecourse students fall into the 19- to 39-year-old age group. Only about 15 percent are in the 40- to 59-year-old group. The latter figures belie the earlier predictions of the open learning advocates in the 1970s. Their feeling then was that many adults over age 40 were only awaiting the opportunity to enroll in college-level courses.

All such data must be assessed within certain contexts. Age ranges and medians vary in accordance with the objectives of the institutions presenting the courses and the nature of the courses themselves. Obviously, the age range of men and women taking National Technological University courses will be reflective of a professional group at the stage of adulthood when people are eager for career advancement. Likewise, people who enroll for credit in a popular Annenberg/CPB Project–supported introductory course in the computer, *The New Literacy,* tend to be somewhat older than students enrolled in an introductory sociology course, with half the enrollments over age 40. Reasons for this are not hard to find. A course like *The New Literacy* is likely to attract people not interested in satisfying basic degree requirements. Indeed, some who take the course already have degrees and are already well established in the world of work. Nowadays, as everyone knows, a passing acquaintance with the computer is either essential or useful to advancement in just about any profession or occupation. On the whole, earlier predictions of the numbers of older adults who were just waiting for chances to take undergraduate courses leading to the bachelor's degree have been pretty well confounded.

Ethnic Background

Ethnic minorities, as already suggested, make up only a small part of enrollments in television-based distance learning projects — no more than 15 percent at most. The reasons to which this can be ascribed are not hard to find. Since, unfortunately, many members of minority groups do not enjoy good living conditions, circumstances simply conspire against their participating in home-study activities. They lack privacy for study at home, must compete with others for access to a single TV set, and are deprived of support from family members. There is also a feeling that distance learning is a second-class route to higher education, rather than an alternative route. Many, too, suffer from the educational deficiencies that make independent study unsuitable for them.

Whatever the reasons, the data available show that television-based study in this country is pretty much a Caucasian activity. As we have seen, the telecourse student viewing lessons at home is likely to be an 18- to 30-year-old white woman. The odds are that she is married and a mother. Her record in high school was good, and she probably ranked in the upper 50 percent of her graduating class. In short, she is the kind of student for whom an academic counselor would predict success in a conventional program of study.

Motivation

In 1977, the Corporation for Public Broadcasting commissioned a survey that told instructional TV practitioners much more than it set out to do.[12] The announced purpose of the study was to determine how *The Ascent of Man* was being adapted to uses as a credit telecourse. This much-acclaimed BBC series, as noted earlier, was converted into a credit ·course and is still used by a fair number of colleges and universities.

Results disclosed that the size of enrollment in user institutions varied with the official course designation assigned to the series by the college. If the telecourse was labeled a humanities or a social science course, or a course satisfying some definite curriculum requirement, credit enrollments were significantly higher than if it was not. Colleges labeling *The Ascent of Man* an elective course satisfying no particular requirement reported low enrollments. This only corroborated what institutions making regular use of telecourses had known for a long time. Telecourse students, as a rule, are attracted not so much by the intrinsic interest of a course's content as they are by whether or not the course helps them move a bit closer to their ultimate academic goals.

This survey produced incontrovertible evidence that students enrolled in distance learning projects are driven by strong credentialing and occupational goals. Many want to improve themselves on the job or eventually earn degrees. They want whatever time and effort they devote to formal study to mean something in realizing their objectives. The motivation of some distant learners is so strong that, according to some investigators, the teaching method or medium employed to reach them is irrelevant, provided it is well used.[13] As Walter Perry once remarked of the BOU's method of teaching, "It is the most difficult way of getting a degree yet invented by the wit of man."

Occupation

Surveys of distance learners often do not seek out detailed information about occupation, but most reveal that blue collar workers are underrepresented in programs of formal study. A 1978 BOU survey disclosed only 10 percent of the students representing recognizable blue collar occupations. (Now that the BOU is moving more toward emphasis on technology and shorter courses of study leading to occupational/technical qualifications, this proportion may change.) This pattern disclosing a preponderant proportion of students in distant learning projects being employed in white-collar occupations holds, as well, in part-time evening divisions in colleges and universities.

The 1984 *Telecourse Student Survey,* mentioned above, revealed another interesting fact about telecourse students and their employment. Most, as would be expected, are employed part or full time. The appeal for the student of a particular telecourse varies with his or her employment status, that is, whether he or she is working part or full time. Those employed full time seem to gravitate toward occupationally oriented telecourses — the courses in business and management currently so popular on campuses, for example. Those employed less than full time are drawn more to general education courses, as are students who are taking conventionally taught courses at the same time they take telecourses — all of which leads us again to the conclusion that distant learners in telecourses have strong motivation and strong goal orientation.

SUMMARY

Experiences with instructional television in higher education have thus far exploded at least one fondly cherished belief. Some adult educators hoped that thousands and thousands of Americans in blue collar jobs would flock to programs that would enable them to earn college degrees in alternative ways. The composite profile that has emerged to date of the typical student enrolled in an undergraduate-level telecourse deflates this meliorist hope. A typical telecourse student turns out to be a duplicate of the man or woman who takes evening courses in a university evening division. One suspects, too, that a disproportionately large number of the people who enroll in a project like the Wayne State University "To Educate the People" Project, established with trade union support and a strong commitment to encourage those who work with their hands to seek further education, represent white collar occupations — civil servants, clerical, and administrative employees.

Television certainly has — and still does — allow some people to take college courses, or more college courses, than they would have if it were not available. TV study, as has been said repeatedly throughout this book, cannot be overestimated as a convenience for the busy adult, the physically handicapped, the institutionalized person, or the person employed at odd hours. Nonetheless, there are really no signs that TV courses, especially of the kind most commonly offered by colleges and universities, are attracting to any significant degree really new student bodies, in particular the intellectually unwashed dreamed of by idealist educators. This seems to be so even in the BOU, located in a country where higher education opportunities have been much more limited than here.

One reality cannot be asserted often enough: college-level telecourses, like other independent study options, presuppose as a condition of success a student with a high level of motivation, adequate academic preparation, and firm career and curriculum goals. Already mentioned are the unwary who mistook TV courses as easy ways to pick up college credits. Completing even a single TV course can be difficult — and apparently study by television is not for everyone.

A WORD ON THE AUDIENCE FOR
INFORMAL ADULT EDUCATION

Some readers may be wondering why so little has been said about adults who want to learn, but have no interest in the academic trappings — passing examinations, earning credits, and so on. Every year, hundreds of thousands of such adults enroll in the noncredit adult education courses offered by secondary schools, college and university extension divisions, and museum and cultural institutions. Many are interested in self-improvement; many simply in broadening their intellectual horizons. In the early 1950s, the Chicago TV College invited viewers to "enroll" as not-for-credit students. In 1956, for example, about 1,500 enrolled in an English composition course on a not-for-credit basis. Foreign language courses attracted many more. A course in Russian when offered for the first time had almost 2,500 not-for-credit enrollees. (This was in the days when the Soviets' space exploits were stimulating not only an interest in science and mathematics, but also an interest in Russian language and culture.)

The question naturally arises as to why adult educators do not design more informal courses for distant learners on television. This in no way implies that PBS, the Annenberg/CPB Project, the Learning Channel, or the community colleges that produce and present telecourses are not serving the informal adult learner admirably. To cite only one example, PBS's *NOVA* represents adult education at its best. Among the viewers of series designed as college-credit courses, there surely are many informal adult learners who tune into programs faithfully and even do some of the prescribed readings, solely out of a simple desire to learn. Why are such viewers not enrolled somehow as "auditors" and permitted to sit in on off-campus classes without taking examinations?

Although the Chicago TV College, as just indicated, accepted noncredit enrollments for a time, the enrollment, in most cases, amounted to little more than a gesture. Informal students paid a slight fee sufficient only to defray the costs of the telecourse study guides sent them. Some purchased textbooks from the bookstores in the Chicago area that stocked TV College textbooks, but for most of them, watching programs was the extent of their participation.

The major obstacle to designing telecourses for uses in noncredit adult education programs is a financial one. Noncredit programs, typically, have to be self-supporting, even in tax-supported institutions. In return for the fees they pay, adult education students expect a series of lectures or discussions and an opportunity for some social interaction. Students of beginning Russian or German, for example, even though they are studying on a noncredit basis, do want some chance to practice the skills they are learning with an instructor. Unfortunately, to design this kind of experience for the noncredit telecourse students would drive fees higher than most would be willing to pay, even if, indeed, many noncredit students would be willing to pay even the most modest fees for adult education on television. High studio production costs, in addition to the expenses of providing the supportive instructional services, make it unlikely that this kind of adult education activity can be provided on open television.

The Chicago TV College did produce several series for use exclusively as noncredit adult education offerings, the most successful of which was a series on careers in real estate. The eight half-hour TV programs featured on-location demonstrations and experts in various phases of real estate operations. In addition, enrollees were invited to several on-campus sessions and took part in a field trip sponsored by a local real estate title insurance agency. Those who participated fully were awarded certificates of completion. A total of 200 students enrolled in the course, which was made possible only because at the time the State of Illinois Community College Board was able to reimburse colleges for certain adult education courses. This state support allowed the TV College to keep the noncredit student fees minimal.

Given production or program acquisition costs, plus the expense of providing follow-up instruction, televised noncredit adult education is feasible only as a by-product of already available materials. For example, whenever the BBC's *The Long Journey,* a first-rate series of programs on comparative religion filmed on location all over the world, is scheduled by a local PBS station or a cable channel, an alert adult educator can build a rewarding program around it. He or she can arrange to have adult education students view the programs at home as they are broadcast or arrange to replay the programs on videocassettes in classrooms or community centers. Besides discussions involving the students themselves, the instructor can also invite in experts from the community — clergymen and scholars. For that matter, if he or she can find the money, the teacher can purchase a set of videocassettes for use on campus or in community centers.

This kind of thing has been, and is being, done. Television, thanks especially to the Annenberg/CPB Project and the BBC, is endowing adult educators with a rich inventory of materials. Rather than waiting for open broadcast opportunities, it is easier, however, for the adult education director to use series like *Civilisation, The Ascent of Man,* and *The Long Journey* in videocassette recordings when they become available for purchase or lease.

Once again, a reader should not conclude that there are no agencies providing noncredit adult, leisure-time, and self-improvement programs on television. One worthy of special notice is the already mentioned The Learning Channel, an outgrowth of the federally funded Appalachian Educational Satellite Project, which now, for a modest per-subscriber fee, provides cable TV systems with informal adult education programming, ranging from "how-to-do-it" series to programs in consumer and general economics. High school and college adult education directors in parts of the country where The Learning Channel is reaching homes have a valuable opportunity to build programs around strands of programming featured on that channel.

New Instructional and Cooperative Patterns

NATIONALIZING CURRICULA

Telecourses that gain such wide adoption as to take on the status of national courses inevitably give rise to fears of "nationalized" courses and curricula. One adult educator, although conceding that off-campus students can receive good instruction "through modern technology" adds the debilitating proviso that any college employing the technology must make use of its own faculty to develop the telecourses used. To adopt for local use a telecourse, say, in anthropology or psychology produced elsewhere, no matter how effective it may be in content or how appealing it is visually, is to risk "the homogenization of instruction" and further the establishment of "national standardized courses . . . stultifying to faculty members and to institutions."[1] Upon reading this, one is immediately tempted to ask if local faculties find the nationally adopted textbooks they use "stultifying."

Most efforts to encourage shared uses of higher education resources or facilities are thwarted by faculties and administrators, even if sharing would eliminate costly duplication. As has been stated repeatedly in these pages, the desire for local autonomy, for putting an institution's own stamp on everything, will not be denied, especially when it comes to the materials of instruction. For this reason, as has also been noted in these pages, designers of telecourses intended for marketing nationwide plan them so that they lend themselves to local modifications.

This is not to say that collaboration, interinstitutional cooperation, or shared uses are rare in higher education. In recent years, whenever certain programs of instruction become prohibitively expensive, we have seen much more shared uses of equipment and personnel. An instance that comes immediately to mind is nuclear physics research, where extremely costly facilities are required. Likewise, colleges and universities committed to telecommunications uses soon recognize the advantages of shared ownership and management of satellite transmission systems. Single institutions usually find it difficult and inefficient to provide the manpower and technological resources needed to operate such systems. It makes much more sense for the American Association of Community and Junior Colleges to construct, manage, and operate a satellite transmission service — as it is about to do — and make the facilities available to its membership of a 1,000 or so two-year colleges on a shared-cost basis.

Thus far, however, the willingness of institutions to cooperate and share resources has extended pretty much to the joint ownership and management of transmission, or delivery, equipment. Despite the great disparities in TV production facilities and skilled production personnel that exist among colleges, there is relatively little sharing in this area. There are notable exceptions, of course, as, for example, in the State of Indiana, where sophisticated statewide telecommunications and production services are available to all public schools and colleges. On the whole, however, colleges and universities tend to resist or remain indifferent to ventures that would afford them shared uses of well-equipped and well-staffed TV production and broadcast outlets managed on an interinstitutional basis.

In the early 1970s, the State of Illinois, as a result of special legislation, planned to organize several regional higher education consortia, each to be centered around comprehensive production and broadcast facilities that would be open to consortia members in a region, as well as to all other public and private institutions. In the populous northern part of the state, the Chicago Metropolitan Higher Education Council (CMHEC), made up of eight or nine two-year and four-year colleges and universities, was established and envisaged as eventually owning and managing a TV station and full-production facility open to all colleges, universities, museums, cultural, scientific, and public service organizations within the region. Negotiations were initiated with officials of Chicago's public TV station for the transfer of the license to operate the disused UHF TV channel it owned but had let fall into a state of disrepair. In the end, for a variety of reasons, political and otherwise, this imaginative plan, which would have placed a first-class TV production facility under interinstitutional academic control, had to be abandoned. First of all, there was fierce competition for the limited funds to be made available in the state's higher education budget for the enterprise. Some of the state institutions simply were indifferent to the plan because of faculty and administrative inertia. Others were suspicious of the new kind of governance it represented. Eventually, the UHF TV channel that was to have been the linchpin of the cooperative project passed over to the control of the City Colleges of Chicago and now functions as the city's second PBS service, presenting among its offerings a schedule of college-level telecourses.

As time has passed, however, more and more colleges have recognized that, if off-campus students are to be afforded instruction on television, they have no choice but to enter into cooperative arrangements with others, if only to have access to high-quality materials at manageable cost. This means acquiring materials collectively. The desire for shared uses of materials produced under Annenberg/CPB Project auspices, or by other producers of quality materials, has prompted formations of new kinds of partnerships among the colleges and universities themselves, as well as between colleges and agencies such as public broadcasters, commercial publishers, cultural organizations, foundations, and business and industrial agencies. Some of these partnerships have been mentioned in passing. It may be useful, however, to glance at them once more in this context.

CONSORTIA AND PARTNERSHIPS

The list of higher education TV/telecommunications associations is an impressive one, and would be treasured by a collector of jaw-breaking acronyms. Community college groups, as might be expected, are the most numerous and active. There are regional, statewide, and national consortia. Just about all of these continuously active regard the collective acquisition of video materials as an important function. Group purchases and leases reduce costs for individual members. Many also regard information-sharing and proselytizing new telecourse users as important activities. This involves orienting faculty to television as an instructional medium and showing them how to utilize it effectively. Some consortia even serve as agencies for the design, production, and distribution of both one-way and interactive telecourses. The State of Oregon Community College Telecommunity College Telecommunications Consortium, The Southern California Consortium for Community College Television, and The Wisconsin Board of Vocational, Technical, and Adult Education are just some notable examples of such regional associations.

The Instructional Telecommunications Consortium (ITC), which has already been referred to several times, is a good example of an active national consortium. An affiliate of the American Association of Community and Junior Colleges, it has as members single- and multi-campus community colleges, four-year colleges and universities, regional and state associations of two- and four-year colleges that employ instructional television and technology, publishing houses, and individual media specialists. This group, really a "consortium of consortia," is international, since its membership includes several Canadian institutions.

The ITC, which began in 1977, is an example of an organization that seemed to spring up in response to the shared need for cooperative action in television and media use. During its first few years, it was a casually organized group of about ten consortia, multi-campus institutions, and single colleges whose principal interest was producing, distributing, and utilizing video courses. Prominent community college producers and national distributors of telecourses — Coastline Community College, The Southern California Consortium, Dallas Community College District, Miami-Dade Community College, Northern Virginia Community College — were among the charter members. Others, although not themselves producers of telecourses, had collaborated with Coastline in the design of its remarkably successful introductory psychology course, *Understanding Human Behavior*. Coastline and Miami-Dade, in addition to having earned reputations as designers and producers of original telecourses with high production values, had also adapted BBC and Time-Life, Inc.–produced video series — *Civilisation* and *The Ascent of Man* are notable examples — for use as college-credit courses both in classrooms and on open television.

Although some of the ITC early members were particularly interested in cultivating and widening the markets for their telecourses, all were keenly interested in how telecourses could be adopted successfully and made satisfying experiences for the new kinds of students colleges were beginning to court. The ITC recognized that the following services were needed: (1) information about telecourses and introducing faculty to their uses; (2) media-based programs of study to help adults who preferred to or had to study off campus to achieve their goals more quickly;

(3) policies for instructional television and instructional telecommunications established at the national level. As the last service suggests, it was no accident that the ITC affiliated with the American Association of Community and Junior Colleges, which is headquartered in Washington, D.C. and, like most national higher education associations, maintains liaison with the Congress and federal agencies. As uses of television in higher education grew, it became apparent that instructional television had to have a voice at the national level, where communications policies were made and national higher education policies were planned and discussed.

In its first years, much of the ITC effort was devoted to the first of the service areas it had mapped out for itself, that is, spreading the word about the usefulness and effectiveness of television as an instructional mode. Two of the ITC's first publications were designed to make colleges aware of the TV courses already available and their usefulness in extension education. *The Catalog of Mass Media College Courses*, first published by the American Association of Community and Junior Colleges in 1978 and revised several times thereafter, attempted to help satisfy what is still a pressing need: providing a reliable guide to telecourses currently available for use as college-level courses. The listing was never intended to be comprehensive, since it limited itself to the undergraduate level and featured mostly the productions of community college producers. Nor was listing in it to be construed as a seal of approval, except in the sense that the courses described therein were designed by their producers for use outside the producing institutions. Other organizations have published more comprehensive catalogs of TV materials for use at all higher education levels. Their usefulness is limited, however, by their being undiscriminating. That is to say, the materials contained range from out-and-out amateurish productions to the sophisticated.

One other widely read early publication was a 1979 collection of articles on telecourses and their uses called *Using Mass Media for Learning*. It appeared just when there was a resurgence of interest in instructional television in higher education.

After four years or so, both the ITC and its parent organization were convinced that the consortium and its services were meeting a real need. One proof of this was that its membership grew steadily. Now, a little more than ten years after it was founded, the ITC is moving steadily toward a roster of a hundred members or so. Since a number of its members are themselves large associations of colleges, the ITC really represents directly and indirectly as many as 400 or more institutions.

Besides supplying timely publications on matters relating to instructional TV and telecommunications uses, the ITC has become a valuable resource for colleges employing telecourses in their programs of instruction. It has conducted in-service workshops for faculty and administrators in regions where active ITC regional committees have been established, and has sponsored forums and discussion sessions on TV use at the annual meetings of national higher education associations. It remains attuned to the concerns of colleges and universities that employ or want to employ telecourses and TV materials.

Since ITC members have as a primary interest presenting credit telecourses, they are very much concerned in developing and maintaining an inventory of courses that permit the serious-minded off-campus students described in an earlier chapter to earn the credits that help them on their way to degree and credentialing goals. Thus, they share the concerns of colleges across the country with adapting some of the Annenberg/CPB Project telecourses to college-credit uses. As noted earlier, a telecourse that may appeal to PBS prime time audiences does not always reflect the content and approach that make it the equivalent of a high-enrollment course on campus.

The ITC also maintained close liaison with the Annenberg/CPB Project staff. To attack the problem just mentioned, Annenberg Project officials funded an ITC project to determine what courses colleges enrolling distant learners felt should be produced. The result was the already cited Annenberg/CPB Project decision to fund production of several courses recommended as needed by representatives of colleges surveyed in the study. These courses, as indicated earlier, will be designed and produced at a level somewhat below that of the Annenberg/CPB courses intended for larger PBS audiences, and are, as also indicated earlier, to be supported in part from preproduction purchases.

The ITC is helpful to institutions interested in instructional video materials in still other ways. Many of them, aware that the supply of high-quality telecourses is uncertain and the right to use such materials often expensive, would like easier access to modestly produced materials, even "talking-face" courses that colleges produce for employment on their own campuses or on local cable TV stations for special-interest audiences (e.g., health care, business, and technical students). The ITC-conducted study of telecourse uses, funded, as noted, by the Annenberg/CPB Project, reveals that of the roughly 250 telecourses surveyed, half are produced by colleges for their own purposes. Others come from institutions that produce courses for use nationwide, accounting for about

30 percent of the telecourses in the survey. A third source of materials are producers of public TV series and corporate training materials, which account for the remainder.[2]

What is significant is that colleges now can arrange to make use of local cable TV channels at little or no cost. Locally produced video, despite its lack of professionalism, is often suitable for showing on cable channels. It is regrettable that much locally made material, which undoubtedly would be useful to colleges other than those who produced it, remains inaccessible. One reason the ITC is currently working with its parent association, the American Association of Community and Junior Colleges, in developing a national community college satellite service is to establish a means of sharing these useful video materials. The satellite will deliver courses and programs to sites all over the country, where they can be recorded for local use via cable, ITFS and videocassette. The community colleges acquiring uplinks will beam materials to the satellite. Community colleges, which place great emphasis on community services and occupational and technical training, will have easy and regular access to useful materials produced by their fellow colleges across the country. With a satellite transmission system in operation, it is to be expected that, within a reasonable time, uplinks to the satellite will be sited at strategic points throughout the country so that more institutions can share their materials with others. Funds for uplink construction are available from federal sources.

With its diverse membership and its broader, nonparochial interests, the ITC holds promise of becoming a model of cooperative services for instructional media users. Whether it will remain, as it has been, a relatively freestanding agency, representing a wide range of postsecondary users of television and other instructional media, or will be swallowed up by its parent organization is another question. Its image as that of a predominantly community college agency may prove in the long run to be unfortunate. What is certain is that there is a real need in the whole of higher education for an agency concerned with educational technology and the relationship between technology and distance teaching and learning.

SPECIALIZED INTEREST ASSOCIATIONS

As new video technologies establish their instructional effectiveness and, more particularly, as they become financially feasible for colleges, cooperative associations with even narrower and more specialized interests appear. Military trainers and researchers at the University of Nebraska and elsewhere, with the aid of an Annenberg/CPB Project award, have shown that the videodisc, because of its adaptability to interactive learning strategies, can be effective for learning tasks that require step-by-step procedures. Videodisc exercises, for example, can help a student simulate hands-on experiments in a science laboratory. The videodisc, which is like an ordinary phonograph record, also has properties that make it an ideal library resource. With a storage capacity of over 54,000 frames, the disc can record conventional video signals, still frames, and print. In fact, the videodisc seems well suited to correspondence study use, should it ever rival the VCR in popularity — which seems unlikely, since unlike the VCR, it does not record programs off the air but plays only prerecorded materials. Yet, an entire college course could be put on both sides of a disc, including video sequences, slides, graphics, and text. Associations of colleges and universities interested in investigating and furthering uses of the videodisc, similar to the group already formed under the leadership of the University of Nebraska, will undoubtedly be emerging. The costs of programming the videodisc, especially for interactive employment, are still so high that collaborative efforts are necessary.

Any new technology, once it is extensively adopted, prompts the formation of new alliances in the higher education community. Thus, the steadily growing use of satellite-delivered teleconferences has spawned interinstitutional organizations of various kinds. Most are multipurpose, in that they provide services for the institutions and groups of institutions that sponsor teleconferences as well as supply information about teleconferencing and its advantages. The services include preproduction, production, and actual broadcast activities. Some of these agencies work closely with certain professional and occupational associations — the U.S. Chamber of Commerce or the American Bar Association, for example. Others have a more general clientele. Worthy of notice are the Public Service Satellite Corporation (PSSC), The National University Teleconference Network (NUTN), and the Adult Learning Satellite Service (ALSS) of PBS. The demand for satellite-delivered TV programming has even encouraged some entrepreneurs to offer colleges and universities special "packages" of services, including educational/ instructional programs, as well as entertainment for students living on campus.

The broadcast satellite, as the general public is aware, is playing an important role in making ours the information age. By virtue of satellite technology, TV viewers all around the world were able to see events in Tiananmen Square in far off Beijing as Chinese students defied their government. The video teleconference, which is regularly used in higher education, routinely links together people far distant from each other for live discussions. Businessmen in Baton Rouge, Louisiana, take part in a panel discussion originating in Washington, D.C. In addition, through telephone or audio connection, they ask questions of a panelist or voice objections to what has been said.

Colleges, universities, and professional and learned organizations regularly employ the video teleconference for a variety of reasons, ranging from administrative briefings to professional development. One useful feature of the teleconference is its timeliness. A legislative development in Washington, D.C., or the state capital can be explored and discussed much more quickly than if a face-to-face meeting were to be scheduled and arranged. The satellite, too, makes it possible for organizations to make use of expertise more efficiently and economically. It is easier, for instance, to bring congressmen and other authorities to a studio, whence their presentations will be transmitted throughout the region or the state, than to have them attend live sessions with the expenses and time required for travel. It should be noted, also, that teleconferencing allows for artful, effective video presentation of topics, providing, of course, sponsors are willing to absorb the costs of preproduction and production costs.

The National University Teleconference Network, or NUTN, is representative of agencies employing satellite transmission for educational/instructional purposes. Its membership is made up of some 250 colleges in this country and in Canada, and its international division links up with institutions outside the United States. It also arranges for conferencing via computer and audio devices. About half the NUTN membership is comprised of community colleges — which is not at all surprising, since these institutions, by virtue of their being scattered throughout their states and because of their dedication to community service, make good reception centers for conferences of interest to community groups — business, industry, health care agencies, the public schools, local and municipal governments.

NUTN gives an individual member a chance to reach national audiences with conferences it originates itself. Every year, it delivers discussions of a wide range of timely topics, from issues in adult education to Medicare. Members are assessed fees for the use of programs, although they are free to participate in programs or not, as they please. The programs to be scheduled are determined by a screening committee or by surveys of the membership.

The satellite has added greatly, and will add even more, to the versatility of distance teaching and community service. With increasing international linkages, the satellite promises to enrich on-campus instruction still more. It has already been noted how some colleges and universities make use of international satellite transmissions to supplement classroom instruction in foreign languages, international affairs, and intercultural subjects. (A group called the Committee for International Tele-Education has already been set up.) Above all, the satellite frees colleges and universities that employ television for the extension of instruction from the tyranny of broadcast schedules. As has been mentioned, the PBS Adult Learning Satellite Service now permits colleges to record telecourses and replay them at suitable times on cable television and in other broadcast modes.

Teleconferencing can be conducted satisfactorily in many cases without video, and with much less fuss and expense. Indeed, colleges, universities, and associations now exchange information both within and outside institutions via personal computer linkages. Others make extensive use of telephone conferencing. Still, the video teleconference has an impact and immediacy that these disembodied media lack, and will continue to find wide and varied uses in higher education.

As this chapter is intended to show, increasing uses of communications technologies and increasing refinements of the technologies themselves have accelerated the formation of partnerships and cooperative arrangements. Alliances between broadcasters and educators will continue, whether or not open broadcast time remains available for colleges and universities. The newer technologies now available will spark other kinds of alliances with broadcast agencies. Even though some readers may shy away from what may seem overly technical terms, note should be taken in passing of certain video transmission devices that have occasioned interesting partnerships. So-called Vertical Blanking Interval (VBI) freeze-frame transmission employs an unused portion of the broadcast signal to carry still video images, as closed caption is carried for the hard of hearing on commercial and PBS stations. (Telephone lines, as a matter of fact, have been utilized for such transmission for over twenty years.) VBI is one way of enhancing audio lectures with slides for students listening in remote classrooms. The Utah State University Extension Division makes use of a Salt Lake City commercial TV station to send slide lectures to locations across the state. A freeze-frame network, Scan Net, has been developed to do such things as bring images of guest experts into classrooms via telephone lines. A senator from Hawaii, for example, can be connected by telephone directly from Washington, D.C., to a classroom at the University of Hawaii — and be visible.

Certainly, partnerships between cable operators and colleges will flourish. That is, the ones in which colleges supply their cable partners with useful, informative programming regularly will prosper. Colleges will also continue to collaborate in producing video materials and in sharing it. Once additional satellite services for transmitting college level materials are easily accessible, there will be even more sharing with others of the video materials colleges now produce for their own local uses.

TELEVISION COMBINED WITH OTHER MEDIA

This study has focused exclusively on the TV medium, but it must not be forgotten that, in distance teaching, the TV medium must be employed in combination with other media if instruction is to be effective. The projects that have maximum impact are multi-media systems incorporating the video technologies, the computer, radio and audiocassettes, the old-fashioned telephone, and, of course, old-fashioned printed correspondence materials.

These combinations result in radically changed teaching techniques in media-based courses. In the years ahead, these media combinations will even reshape conventional instruction, especially as combinations of video and print such as *The Story of English* (a telecourse now used by students both on- and off-campus) result in a new kind of textbook. Above all, telecourse team design, as described in an earlier chapter, already has had some influence on course planning, especially on campuses where telecourses are used. The team design of telecourses, involving specialists in the academic disciplines, instructional designers, and TV producers, provides a model, albeit an expensive and time-consuming one, for college teachers looking for ways to improve their teaching, particularly at the introductory undergraduate level. In any event, teachers who have served as members of teams designing telecourses, usually report that they return to their classrooms with fresh and new ideas for making their teaching fresher and more imaginative.

Likewise, as we have seen, television has been the occasion for much fruitful cooperation within higher education itself. It is encouraging more frequent and more productive contacts between colleges and universities and their communities.

One of the enduring values of higher education is that it opens windows for inquiring minds. Television, too, at its best, opens windows on the world. It can be a powerful weapon in the arsenal of higher education.

The Future of Television in Higher Education

Predictions, forecasts, crystal ball consultations, whatever they are called, are always risky, and the risk becomes particularly high when it comes to foreseeing changes in higher education practices. The ears of some college teachers who were teaching in the late 1950s and 1960s may still be ringing with the confident pronouncements of various enthusiasts and promoters that a new day was dawning, when old-fashioned and discredited teaching methods would be displaced by assorted teaching machines and programmed learning texts. Students would soon be fed bits of information in frames, or units, so easily digestible that chances of failure would be precluded. Specialists calling themselves educational technologists were proclaiming that TV monitors and computer screens would soon be taking the place of live teachers, and that the live teachers would never be missed.

Still others, as has already been indicated, argued that a challenging new age was arriving for higher education, the age of nontraditional, open, or distance teaching. Speakers at meetings and conventions of telecommunications associations predicted that as many as 7 or 8 percent of the total adult population were potential enrollees in TV courses alone. Unfortunately, most colleges adopting telecourses were lucky if twenty-five off-campus students enrolled in them. Quickly, some American educators concluded that television-based distance teaching projects in this country were completely unlike the BOU, in that they did not fill an educational void. American adults are unlike their counterparts abroad in that they have the luxury of plentiful higher education opportunities.

Open-door community colleges are within their reach in most areas of the country, public school systems offer adult education programs, and college and university extension and evening divisions are not in short supply. Certainly, there are adults who are candidates for the television-based kinds of distant learning projects described in earlier pages. However, it soon became clear that even the most successful projects in areas with heavy population concentration could regard only 2 percent of the adults at most as potential enrollees.

Unfortunately, one of the handicaps advocates of TV instruction, as well as champions of other modes of electronically based instruction, struggle under is the unbridled enthusiasm of some colleagues as to the efficacy of the TV medium and the size of the audiences for televised instruction. From its earliest days, instructional television has been plagued by well-meaning, but overly zealous, promoters. Some of this zeal stems from distributors' needs to encourage colleges and universities to lease or purchase materials produced at considerable cost, but the promotion in the past has often struck faculties, especially those in four-year colleges and universities, as hucksterism. In recent years, however, now that telecourses have established a respected place for themselves, there has been less abrasiveness in promotion. Perhaps, too, more colleges and universities, driven by exigencies of declining enrollments, having themselves resorted to professional marketing techniques in their quest for new sources of students, have found that "selling" is not necessarily offensive.

Often, too, forecasts about video technology uses are made on the basis of misleading assessments of the cost to potential users. Interactive videodisc is a case in point. There is great demand, particularly in skills-training programs, for interactive media-based programs that require a student to become an active learner and respond actively to the material being presented. For this reason, computerized approaches are much in favor with industrial and military trainers. The videodisc is attractive because, in combination with the computer, it allows students to respond by touching keypads or screens, and control their progress from one unit to the next. At this time, the costs of designing sequences for the disc, as well as other equipment costs, are still so high as to put the technology beyond the reach of many colleges. As a result, the videodisc is finding most use in corporate and military training programs.

Video-interactive media, on the whole, come at relatively high prices. To show how expectations can outrun realities, we can look to Japan, where in the 1980s the Japanese government underwrote an elaborate interactive system, named HI-OVIS, which its developers called "the telecommunications system of the 21st century."[1] The fiber-optics-based technology itself typifies what futurists tell us may be commonplace in American homes in the next century, although less sanguine spirits may find it uncomfortably suggestive of some of George Orwell's grimmer predictions in his *1984*. A Japanese home taking part in the project was equipped with a color TV set, a small video camera mounted above the set, a directional microphone to allow a viewer of the set to talk back to the broadcast source, and a console to control the interaction. By depressing an appropriate key in the console, a viewer interrupted and asked a question of a professor lecturing in a classroom of a university in the area. (The home viewer's image and voice were seen and heard in the classroom.) By pressing another key and punching out a code, he or she called up a videotaped program the viewer had selected from a catalog to watch on one of the forty channels of the system. Once the code was received in the control room, a robot arm was dispatched to fetch a videocassette and load it into a player — all in about one minute.

The ministry that furnished households with the equipment hoped that householders would be willing to purchase the materials on their own, at a cost of several thousand dollars. Lack of public response, however, prompted the discontinuance of the project.

No doubt, we can look forward to still newer telecommunication marvels of the HI-OVIS variety. There seems to be a law requiring that technological progress proceed at an ever-accelerating rate. At present, in fact, enough equipment is long since available — cable TV systems, video and audiocassette recorders, personal computers connected by modems and telephone lines to other personal computers — to make the American home a learning center at far from extravagant cost. Unfortunately, the "software" needed to fuel the technological hardware does not follow the law of acceleration. One of the major problems for users of television-based instruction at present is lack of access to usage materials. This seems destined to be a problem in the immediate future at least.

Despite the hazards of looking into the future, it is only fitting to end a study of how television has and is being used in higher education by asking how it will be used over the next several decades. The persistent question was just raised as to where the "software" or instructional programs will come from. What kinds of programs are there likely to be more of? Who will underwrite them?

Will television remain primarily a means to extend instruction to adults studying off campus? Will it make any really significant impact on the shape of instruction on campus? How will it affect print correspondence instruction? Will it become a catalyst or agent for any meaningful changes in adult education?

Before we address ourselves to these questions, however, perhaps it would be helpful to look back to experiences of the last twenty-five or thirty years, and see how they may point to the future. What have we learned? How can what has been learned be of help to those shaping future directions?

PAST EXPERIENCE AS A GUIDE

Planners of television-based instructional projects are often guided more by their own presuppositions than they are by the experiences of those who have employed television in higher education. Indeed, some observers are often struck by how heedless of the findings of others some project directors are. For example, as we have stated several times already, it has long been apparent that, unless a sizable population base made up of adults with certain characteristics be present, a project will not attract enough enrollees to make it self-supporting. The "certain" characteristics of successful distant learners have been known for some time. Twenty years ago, it became obvious that college-level distant learners were willing to sacrifice their time, effort, and convenience because they were in pursuit of credentialing. For this reason, courses not usable in satisfying common curriculum requirements did not attract them. Yet, as we have seen, directors of projects and telecourse producers continue to ignore this and develop curriculum offerings in what can only be described as capricious ways.

Whatever projections are made here about the future should be made on a foundation of what past experiences have taught us. Preceding chapters have sketched the activities of U.S. colleges and universities involved in television-based instruction. As we anticipate future lines of development, it will be helpful to recall some of the lessons that have been learned.

Lessons Learned

In speculating about future developments, it must be kept in mind that television-based instruction in this country has been, up until now, an extension of the conventional higher education system. It is likely to remain the same in the years ahead. The telecourse, perhaps the greatest achievement to date in U.S. multi-media distance education, has given many American adults entry to the higher education system. Distinctive learning experiences as they are, telecourses are still designed to be the equivalents of conventionally taught college courses, convertible into the standard academic coinage of credit hours listed on student transcripts. What is particularly striking is the number of students enrolling in conventional on-campus college courses and telecourses concurrently. Able students apparently can adapt easily to whatever is nonconventional about the telecourse.

Distance educators with a commitment to the employment of video technologies and other media should by now have learned a number of things from the experience of projects in this country, as well as of the BOU. For one thing, there can no longer be any doubt that the mass media, television in particular, are tools that educators can employ to bring high-quality learning materials to audiences, different in demographic and other characteristics from students of conventional college age.

Experience has shown, too, that video as used in the currently standardized telecourse has built-in limitations that make it more suitable for instruction in some areas than in others. Unless it can somehow be so designed as to permit students to interact directly with the course materials, it lends itself more readily to the social sciences, the humanities, and areas like business that can be presented in illustrated lectures. If the predictions of sociologists and economists prove to be sound, and the next century sees people in the developed nations not only living longer and more productively, but also changing occupations throughout their lives, it will be essential that more instructional television be interactive. Television will join forces more and more with the computer in simulating hands-on, job-training experience. Increasingly, as emphasis shifts to the teaching of occupational skills, interactive approaches will become of greater importance. In a 1989 interview, Walter Perry states that the BOU, established originally, as noted, to give adults a chance to earn degrees, will in the future be concerning itself more with re-educating and retraining workers in new job skills.[2] We need think only of the occupational areas now being transformed by micro-electronics to appreciate the need for interactive video in training programs.

Past experience has also shown that effective uses of television in higher education necessitate partnerships. Genuinely interactive approaches that will be required for skills training and retraining in the years ahead will prompt even more alliances between academic institutions on one side and business, industry, professional organizations, and governmental agencies on the other. This is so because the costs of providing such skills-specific training will be too much for the colleges themselves, or may be deemed inappropriate for colleges to assume on their own. There will be more contractual agreements between colleges and outside organizations for the design by the former of interactive video-related educational and training programs. In the advanced-level higher education community, more institutions like the National Technological University will spring up in response to needs in certain industries — computer management, robotics, technological services administration, and the like. Cynical as it may be to say, is it not even possible that, if colleges and universities experience enrollment problems, high-minded faculties may become less resistant to partnerships of the kinds just suggested?

More of the Same — and Even Better

It seems safe indeed to assume that the years immediately ahead will see increased usages of video technologies for continuing occupational and professional education. Professional certification boards are likely to demand even more continuing professional development as skills become obsolete quickly and knowledge goes out of date. Lawyers, doctors, and other well-paid professionals will still prefer to attend week-long seminars on the island of Maui, but accelerating rates of change in professional and technical knowledge and ever-soaring travel costs will make video teleconferencing more and more popular. After all, a video teleconference can be set up fairly quickly in response to professional development needs as they arise. Participation in a teleconference is much less expensive than a trip to Hawaii.

Even though video conferences can be set up quickly to meet pressing problems, if they are to find wider and lasting acceptance, their organizers and managers will have to give them higher production values. Audiences will tolerate much more boredom from live speakers, if only because they are physically present, than they will from images on the TV screen. This was commented on during the discussion of the ill-fated uses by universities of closed-circuit television to alleviate earlier problems caused by heavy student enrollment and shortages of faculty. As already noted, there are now people who are specialists in planning and producing teleconferences (which, it must be remembered, can run for several hours) so that they are well-paced, with well-lighted sets, attractive graphics, and so on. Improvements have been made in the presentation of graphics, for example, with devices like the video inserter that allow a speaker to display graphics on an auxiliary monitor. Thus, as he or she speaks and is seen on one monitor in a conference room, the graphic display appears on another.

There seems to be little question that special services like the Stanford University Network and the National Technological University will continue to flourish. That is, there will be more demands for services that deliver instruction directly from the campus classroom to work and corporate viewing sites. The current shift from a heavy industrial to a service base in the American economy will, as has been stated, entail that adults, once their job skills are no longer in demand, be retrained in service-related areas. Much of this training can be delivered by the community colleges, once they have easy access to their satellite transmission system now being developed and form an occupational/technical skills training network. Some of the training, which, by the way, need not always carry formal academic credit, can come from the agencies mentioned earlier that provide training programs for corporate employees — agencies like the PBS National Narrowcast Service. Such programming, of course, designed for audiences including sizable numbers of involuntary viewers, would profit greatly from production qualities much higher than those of classroom lectures designed for well-motivated viewers. A problem for services like the PBS National Narrowcast Services will be locating and acquiring up-to-date, high-quality materials in sufficient quantity.

What has just been said about involuntary viewers of in-service training programs brings us back to the person mentioned in an earlier section, the man or woman who has no interest in credentials or certificates, but is interested in learning in an informal way. It is easy to overestimate the number of people who would watch solely out of personal interest TV programs on managing their personal finances, running small businesses, or living healthier lives. In the years when cable TV companies were vying for franchises in communities and municipalities all over the country, community groups and franchising authorities demanded that the would-be franchisees provide special channels — and even production equipment — dedicated to community services and adult learning. Much of this proved to be a will-o'-the-wisp, because some of the cable operators never made good on their promises, and if they did, local colleges and universities, cultural organizations, and business and health agencies could not supply enough programming to put together satisfactory, nonredundant schedules for channels.

Colleges and universities that now present telecourses on open and cable television are, of course, serving informal learners. We know that many viewers follow telecourses in economics, business, or philosophy solely out of general interest. Officials of TV College always reckoned that, for every telecourse credit student, there were roughly ten noncredit, or informal, viewers. This does not add up to an audience worthy of the commercial broadcaster's notice, but by other standards, it is impressive. It seems likely, given the cooperation of cable operators, that more colleges and universities will emulate the institutions, many of them community colleges, now using cable television to reach informal and formal learners. With a manageable initial investment that would equip a classroom for cablecasting, a university, for example, could bring into local homes the lectures of articulate professors in courses of interest to the general public. The same universities could offer college-level study to advanced-level high school students in the same way. Television gives colleges and universities, whether public or private, the chance to establish themselves as helpful presences and remove the barriers separating them from their communities.

THE PROSPECTS FOR DEGREE-DIRECTED CURRICULA ON TELEVISION

Despite all that has been said about the differences between BOU distant learners and those in this country, one is still tempted to speculate as to whether there will ever appear a national, regional, or statewide institution to allow distant learners to earn the bachelor's degree by way of television and other media-based instruction. As we have seen, there have been proposals for an "American Open University" that would be in effect a credit-brokering agency to make it possible for an adult to earn a degree through credit from a variety of sources, including other institutions, life experiences, proficiency examinations, and independent and nonconventional study. In addition, there are in fact institutions that now allow students to complete degree requirements in nonconventional ways. (The shady "universities" that advertise advanced degrees for all kinds of independent study in airlines' in-flight magazines are not included.) Students have already begun to earn graduate degrees through the National Technological University, but this institution, as we have seen, occupies a special position. Other universities as well now enable distant learners to earn master's degrees in the business area via courses televised from classrooms. In fields like engineering and business administration, there is consensus as to what courses are the components of degree programs.

Unfortunately, in this country the matter of presenting a bachelor's degree curriculum on television is much more complicated. A glance at a representative college catalog shows that the bachelor's program is made up, typically, of a brace of general-education courses, plus elective courses left to the student's option, and a concentration of courses in a field of major interest. One solution might be to devise a distinctive curriculum for adult TV students leading to a generalist kind of bachelor's degree, but experience suggests that not enough American students would opt for this kind of distance study to warrant the effort, even if an effort could be made. Students now enrolling in telecourses gravitate, as we have seen, to the curricula, largely career-directed, that on-campus students favor.

Degrees earned in totally unconventional ways bear a stigma in this country and elsewhere no doubt. For that reason alone, it makes more sense to encourage adults who must look for distant learning opportunities to fulfill formal study goals to combine nonconventional with conventional instruction. As we have seen, that is already happening, particularly in the community colleges, where more and more part-time students mix classroom and televised instruction. The future probably will see producers designing and maintaining a telecourse inventory that will enable a serious distant learner to complete as much as two years of a degree program via television. As we have seen, there already exists a fairly extensive repertory of usable telecourses. If the Annenberg/CPB Project is reinstated and is willing to continue its support of high student demand lower-division courses, and if the practice of inviting institutions to purchase rights to courses in advance of production proves that there are enough users, adult learners may soon be able to complete significant portions of degree programs at home and in libraries.

Some readers may conclude that the bulk of enrollments in this inventory of telecourses will come through community colleges. Community colleges are open to innovative practices. Besides, their fees are usually modest or low as compared to those of four-year colleges and universities. Unfortunately, however, especially for the self-esteem of their producers, students do not seem to value telecourses as highly as conventionally taught courses. For many, they are a second choice. This was shown when the introduction of even nominal tuition charges in the California and Chicago community colleges resulted in immediate and significant drops in enrollments. The telecourses do not seem worth paying for.

It does not help the cause of television as a means of extending higher education if higher educators and the general public associate telecourses almost exclusively with community colleges. Perhaps in the future, state and regional authorities may see an advantage in offering telecourses to distant learners on a wider than a single institutional base. Colleges and universities within an area might jointly sponsor a telecourse schedule on cable TV channels, with a firm agreement that a student earning credit in a course could transfer it to any other of the participating institutions. Each participant would further agree to accept enrollments in at least one of the courses. Most importantly, a common tuition rate would be established for credit enrollment. Once higher education at every level is actively involved, televised instruction will take on greater academic credibility.

SPECIAL AUDIENCES

As already noted, the newer video technologies allow colleges and other training agencies to target audiences with specialized program needs. It was also noted that the nature of the target audience determines the quality of the resulting programming. A course in French or Spanish language and culture that hopes to win a relatively large viewing audience must have high entertainment value, but a course aimed at the relatively few who want to learn a specific occupational skill need not be elaborately produced. The future, one hopes, will provide steady streams of programming of both varieties. It certainly is predictable that, given the technology now available and the demand for programs, much more will be available for special-interest audiences. It can also be anticipated that delivery options for special-interest audiences will continue to increase. Along with the already established means — ITFS, microwave, cable "institutional networks" — now developing capabilities such as addressable cable channels and low-power television will make it easier for instructional designers to target audiences with more precision.[3] Satellite networks like that projected by the American Association of Community and Junior Colleges will serve as distribution outlets for usable learning materials produced at modest cost.

The prospect of producing more materials in a straightforward, didactic style does not necessarily gladden the hearts of those who see the medium as more than a means of extending classroom teaching, that is, as a way of reshaping instructional methodologies. For that matter, no one can deny that well-produced training programs that exploit all the presentational properties of television are effective with audiences at all levels of motivation and maturity. However, is it realistic to hope that the supply of such materials, expensive to produce, can ever satisfy the demand for training and retraining programs as our economy is transformed? Would it not be wasteful not to take advantage of TV technologies now available to extend the resources of conventional higher education to the adult work force and the business and industrial worlds?

SOURCES OF PROGRAMS

Glowing predictions can be made as to the technology. It is certain, too, that colleges will continue to produce instructional TV materials that supplement classroom and laboratory work for students. It is reasonable to assume that more will be willing than at present to make studios of their classrooms so as to bring instruction to people in remote locations. Yet, what about programs for students of conventional college age, like those who showed so little enthusiasm for closed-circuit TV teaching? What about those who, as was stated earlier, are most likely to drop out of telecourses for other than personal or family reasons? Will anything be done for the younger and less motivated learners, the ones in need of higher TV production qualities if their attention is not to wander?

There is the further question, of course, as to how "high" production qualities have to be. Some designers and producers, as has been stated, blunt instructional effectiveness by consciously striving for the production qualities of commercial television. The entertainment features get in the way of instruction for the serious-minded learner. This issue is a difficult one for those interested in using television as a directly educative force. Students watching a program in geology or psychology on Tuesday morning may very well have viewed exciting episodes of *L.A. Law* or *Mission Impossible* the evening before. Television of this kind is so pervasive in their lives that they associate television with fast action, excitement, and total sensory immersion. Marshall McLuhan may have been given to overstatement, but he was not exaggerating when he reminded us that television has changed our lives and our very thought processes. It has accustomed us, especially the young who have grown up with it, to losing ourselves in its real-life sights and sounds. Herein lurks a danger: the exciting images of reality television pours out can distort reality. Television "reality" can be little more than spectacle, fast moving and titillating, but basically uninformative and without significance. It can dull the critical senses and, as some skeptical of the instructional effectiveness of television argue, can render viewers intellectually passive. The result is that viewers can be deluded into believing that learning is easy.

In the future, because of the technological options mentioned, we shall see fewer attempts to court both audiences interested in generally educative programs and ones interested in directly instructional programs. Perhaps the best place for the instructional producer to look for guidance is the consumer, the student. As reported earlier, a sample of Chicago TV College students made it clear that they preferred combinations of production techniques. The highly visual documentary, with its series of images tied together by narration, is effective in that it captures viewers' imaginations and carries them along pleasurably, but ultimately, a teacher is needed on the screen, whether he or she be a real professor or a convincing actor, to summarize, synthesize, point to significances— in short, to supply direct instruction.

Community colleges and agencies like the National Technological University that provide specialized education and training will no doubt continue to bring instruction to special audiences at home and the work place. However — and here is a key question — will there be sources for telecourses of the kind that distant learners are now viewing on the PBS Adult Learning Service? Can we assume that an agency like the Annenberg/CPB Project will be on the scene to underwrite sophisticated productions? For that matter, will the community college producers now helping to supply the national market with high-quality courses be able to carry on?

THE "LOOK" OF THE VIDEO IN EXTENSION INSTRUCTION

It seems almost ironic, in view of what has been said about student resistance to "talking faces," to say that this kind of production will play an important part in postsecondary distance education in the future. Given the equipment and facilities now available to colleges at modest cost, and given the increasing numbers of people who will seek instruction off campus, there will be greater demand for extending classroom instruction. The recently announced Annenberg/CPB Project plan, described earlier, to provide awards to colleges willing to employ telecommunications resources at their disposal to deliver instructional services to students off campus seems a step in the direction of satisfying this demand. Other funding agencies may be moved to follow suit and supply additional incentives for colleges to extend their services to more people through the telecommunications media already accessible to them, including the video technologies, of course. Audiences for resulting programming will not, however, be the captive ones for the closed-circuit television of the 1950s and 1960s, but instead will be made up of men and women in need of specialized education and training.

Instructional television will continue to be pretty much what one critic notes it has been in the past: (1) a master teacher; (2) a means of imparting the real world to the learner; and (3) a complement to the curriculum.[4] Using television to extend the classroom to adults involves the first of the functions just listed. This does not mean that the master teacher must be a "master" in the sense of the early days of instructional television, when it was hoped that the teacher on the screen would serve as a model for less experienced and less talented colleagues. Nor does it mean at the university level that he or she must be a renowned scholar or scientist. Rather, all it means is that a TV host-teacher will be an articulate person, qualified in the subject, and able to organize and present material skillfully enough to be delivered to advanced high school students, graduate-level nurses and health science people, and on-the-job trainees, wherever they happen to be watching.

As for the remaining two functions of instructional television listed above, bringing the outside world to the learner and enriching the curriculum, telecourses of the kind distant learners expect to see on the PBS Adult Learning Service, on The Learning Channel, or on the community college schedules on cable television will continue to perform these services. Where the resources needed will come from is another question. Producers will have to find and devise new and more reliable ways of underwriting the high costs of video productions.

Perhaps the advanced-purchase plan now being tested by a group of community college producers to raise funds to match an award from the Annenberg/CPB Project for producing several high-enrollment telecourses — but at a level of production somewhat below that of the Project courses targeting large general audiences — will prove a feasible way of helping underwriting expenses. As already indicated, this plan is an adaptation of one employed for some years with great success by the Agency for Instructional Television (AIT) of Bloomington, Indiana, which produces instructional TV materials for use in elementary and secondary schools. AIT solicits advance subscriptions to production projects from U.S. state education authorities, as well as from Canadian provinces. The states and provinces determine what the topics of the annual projects are to be, and in return for their contributions, which are scaled to the size of school populations involved, participate in content planning and have unrestricted use of the materials produced. AIT production needs, however, are not as great or as varied as those of college-level producers, being restricted to periodic major enterprises that serve common curriculum needs in broad population bases. Developing and keeping up to date an inventory of video-based, college-level courses will demand extensive and continuous production efforts. Further, the quantity of materials needed precludes top-quality production for every course. Instead, less elaborate and less expensive approaches on some occasions are mandatory, if a supply of usable courses is to be maintained. In addition, it would seem that a larger advance-subscription base than that now in place among community colleges must be cultivated. A substantial number of institutions other than the two-year colleges will have to take part in prepurchasing usage rights if production expenses are to be underwritten without significant help from outside.

There is also the likelihood that in the future costly video will make up a smaller proportion of the total telecourse than it does currently, particularly in the telecourse model that has been standardized by community college producers and users. As we have seen, the BOU found itself steadily reducing the TV component in its instructional method, if only because of escalating video production costs. For that matter, there is really no compelling instructional reason for incorporating twenty-six to thirty half-hour video programs in every telecourse. From what we have discovered about students who profit from telecourses, we know that the courses must be composites of nonelectronic and electronic media. In plain language, most of the instructional load is carried by print, which in no way detracts from the important affective, pacing, and enriching roles played by video.

Patterns and practices do not always come about because of some internal necessity. Sometimes they come about because of entirely extraneous factors. The number of video programs that has become typical of the telecourses presented on the PBS Adult Learning Service every week was not set because designers felt that, without that number, learning outcomes would be impaired. It came about in part because some faculty members argued that there had to be some way to compensate for the time the conventional student spends sitting in a classroom. Time spent viewing television is the nearest equivalent to "seat time." It became a question of how many TV programs approximate the hours a student attends class during a term. In the early days of college-level instruction television, some faculties insisted that a telecourse contain as many as forty-five half-hour video programs. Eventually, as they recognized that TV presentations require tighter organization of materials, they accepted thirty half-hours. That figure, in time, was pared down even more.

Another reason for the number of programs that has become a standard is that, as noted earlier, many courses are still designed for showing on open television. A college offering a course or set of courses on a PTV station usually must request a block of air time that parallels as closely as possible a term of the regular academic schedule. It is easier for a station manager to schedule a series of programs every week over a fourteen- or fifteen-week period than to schedule courses containing varying numbers of programs.

With the newer technologies and the flexibility of scheduling they provide — cable television in particular— it is likely that even fewer hours of open-air time on PBS stations will be available to most colleges and universities. Whether this happens or not, the hard reality seems to be that the video component of the more elaborate productions will be reduced, whenever this can be done without affecting instructional effectiveness. Telecourses in less easily visualizable subject areas, mathematics, for example, can be effective with, perhaps as few as a half-dozen video programs. The objectives of a course in sociology or fine arts, on the other hand perhaps, are realizable only with twenty-six programs.

VIDEO AND OLD-FASHIONED CORRESPONDENCE STUDY

It seems likely that video will give old-fashioned correspondence study a new vigor. The presence of VCRs in so many homes and the ease with which cassettes can be sent through the mail make it feasible for writers to enrich the content of their courses with visual materials. Besides, the video recordings can be of any length, from five minutes to two hours, since they will not be played on open or cable broadcast. How important the role of video will be is difficult to foresee because of the expense of producing video of acceptable quality and the consequent increase in cost to the student.

In addition, video-related study materials distributed by proprietary institutions will be primarily in vocational/technical subjects, where, to be most effective, they should be interactive. Inevitably, this will involve the computer-controlled videodisc. As noted earlier, some interactive programs are now available on both videocassette and videodisc. Because of their high costs, these materials are marketed mainly to corporate users. In fact, media-based correspondence teaching materials in technical areas may remain largely in the hands of corporate trainers.

In this connection, brief mention must also be made of nonpictorial TV delivery methods. Everyone who watches closed-circuit and cable TV channels is acquainted with *Teletext*, the one-way text carrying weather forecasts and announcements. The text is transmitted as part of a broadcast or cable signal. *Videotext*, however, is interactive and is sent on telephone lines or by way of two-way cable systems. The generic term for both text and graphical information is *Electronic Text*. (To add to the confusion of a layman, there is no general agreement on how the terms are used.) An advantage of electronic text from the instructional standpoint is that it can be "downloaded," or stored, in a personal computer for later use once a transmission has ended.

A demonstration grant from the Annenberg/CPB Project permitted a team from San Diego State University, the University of Wisconsin, and the University of Nebraska to investigate the potential of electronic text in college level instruction. Some electronic text materials were designed — such as self-quizzes, games, and so on — to supplement a PBS series called *Understanding Your Investments*. The PBS station licensed to the University of Nebraska has even developed three freestanding courses for an interactive cable system. The official report on this Annenberg/CPB Project demonstration is less than optimistic, conceding that there is "much work ahead" in finding direct instructional uses for electronic text, or in employing it in "enhancing other materials" — telecourses, for example.[5] Observers less beguiled by technology might be tempted to inquire if electronic self-quizzes or games are any more effective than ones that are mimeographed or Xeroxed. Observers with an even more irreverent attitude toward the technology might object that electronic text is only print that is not imprinted on the pages of a book. A book has the inestimable advantage of being easier to read and hold.

TELEVISION AND THE
COLLEGE/UNIVERSITY CURRICULUM

The title of this subsection may sound presumptuous or naive — or both. The topic announced might very well be the topic of an essay or book by a cultural critic, a historian, or even a professor of education. In a sense, too, the effects of television are so obvious as to preclude comment here. An English student of mass communication, Richard Hoggart, has commented that television makes viewers aware of "a range of worthwhile interests and pleasures far wider than most of us would otherwise have known." Through television, Public Television in particular, college and university students have the opportunity to see informed discussions of public issues; to see and hear noteworthy people who, before television, would have been merely names to them; to watch musical performances; and to have aesthetic experiences that would otherwise have been beyond their ken.

As commentators are so fond of pointing out, television is a powerful and pervasive force in our society. Today's students may have a shaky hold on geography, but through television the world has become their "global village," to use Marshall McLuhan's by now hackneyed phrase. Young Americans sit in classrooms in North Carolina or Oregon and discuss problems they have in common with contemporaries sitting in classrooms in France and Germany. Young Americans studying Russian or French watch and hear newscasts and commentaries by native speakers of these languages emanating from the Soviet Union and France. Americans of all ages saw history the moment it was being made as students squared off with tanks in Tiananmen Square in Beijing, or in Germany as young Germans stormed and dismantled the Berlin Wall. All this came as the result of TV signals transmitted by orbiting satellites.

Educators, of course, will assert that television's effects are not always desirable. How often have we heard recited the depressing statistics about the hours children spend before TV sets before they even enter school? High school and college students, we are told, spend four or five hours a day with their eyes glued to TV screens. Some teachers, in desperate attempts to arouse their students' interest, even try to turn this addiction to advantage by making popular TV programs subjects of investigation, often making believe that cheap soap operas are as worthy of the same kind of analysis as serious drama.

However deplorable the effects of television may be on college students' attention spans, reading habits, reading competencies, values, and perceptions of reality, they are matters for another kind of book. What is relevant here is that the age of the book's domination for entertainment and information has come to an end. Even before television's rise as the most popular mass medium, radio and film took up a good deal of the time of the average citizen. The following statement was not made by an overexcited audiovisualist, but by a highly respected scholar and literary critic:

> The graphic impact of television, the information-load which can be gathered swiftly and accurately by the new electronic media, is such that in many respects the book today is antiquarian, as luxurious an instrument as was the illuminated manuscript after Gutenberg. The "library" of tomorrow will, to a very large degree, be a complexity of electronic sources and means of reception in which cable-television is bound to play a major role.[6]

With television's triumph, the newspaper and magazine have gone into decline. Most Americans, it is safe to say, now rely on television, with its inchoate streams of images and disjointed bits of information, for their knowledge of world affairs.

Whether this is a state of affairs to be deplored or welcomed is of little moment, since it has come about and is unlikely to be reversed. For that matter, the picture and the graphic illustration began to challenge text well before television invaded living rooms. To confirm this, all anyone whose formal school experiences took place before World War II need do is leaf through the pages of a current high school or college undergraduate textbook. The copious graphics, illustrations, photographs, layout, and color scheme are a far cry from the dense, unbroken thickets of text of their old school books. In justification, contemporary educational psychologists claim that there is evidence that pictures help students recall information. Then, too, the heavy bombardment of visual imagery to which the youth are subjected every day of their lives makes them shy away from solid pages of print.

In all fairness, it must be remembered that arguments can be made on the other side. That is, we can contend that television helps the cause of reading. PBS viewers following a series of illustrated lectures on world history, distributed by the admirable South Carolina Educational Television network, are invited to send off for a companion text. Many do, no doubt. When PBS stations across the nation presented an adaptation of German novelist Thomas Mann's classic *Buddenbrooks*, stacks of the paperback edition of the novel appeared in bookstores around the country. The BBC's adaptation of Evelyn Waugh's *Brideshead Revisited*, which also appeared on PBS, led to the sale of a half-million copies of the novel in paperback. TV performances of operas, concerts, ballets, and plays stimulate interest in attending live performances, just as telecasts of baseball and football games do not keep people away from stadiums but draw them to the live spectacles.

Video and book seem to complement each other naturally. Certainly a TV program alone cannot rival the printed page as a way of conveying analytical thought. For one thing, the book is always under the control of its reader, who can linger over a passage to ponder or savor it, or can turn back to an earlier passage to refresh the memory or check a detail. Television, with all its visual impact, remains on the surface. A student of the American Civil War finds that Matthew Brady's contemporary photographs add a rich human dimension to his or her study, just as the video programs of *The Story of English*, the already-mentioned telecourse now in use in colleges and universities, provide a valuable supplement by letting the student see and hear speakers of varieties of English in their own locale. However, to probe, seek causes, and explore motive, the student must have a text.

How much television is to be blamed for a decline in literacy among higher education students is difficult, if not impossible, to assess. There are other causes to which it can be attributed with as much justification, most of which stem from the school and the family. Thoughtful Americans would agree with E. D. Hirsch, Jr., who in his much-discussed and timely book, *Cultural Literacy: What Every American Needs to Know* (1987), concludes: "It will not do to blame television for the state of our literacy. Television watching does reduce reading and often encroaches on homework. Much of it is admittedly the intellectual equivalent of junk food."[7] Still, despite the "junk food" quality of much of commercial TV programming, the medium itself possesses properties of undeniable value for instruction.

We can expect, therefore, to see video being wedded to print in ways other than telecourses. Textbooks and workbooks supplemented by video programs will not be uncommon in the years ahead. Publishers will design video programs, some as short as ten or fifteen minutes, to illustrate concepts, demonstrate techniques, motivate, and so on. This means more students will learn more on their own.

Throughout this book, however, reference has been made to inter-activity as a way of making video-based instruction more effective. As has been noted as well, industrial and military trainers, in particular, stress interaction in learning, since their purpose is teaching their students how to do things and how to acquire skills at a mastery or near-mastery level. The computer will be a key tool in this mode of instruction. The microcomputer opens access to a whole new world of information. As one telecommunications specialist put it: "Couple the home computer with the telephone as well as with television, and a new storehouse of information is unlocked."[8]

Although it has not yet really caught on because, among other things, of the high costs of designing instructional programs for it, one can only conclude that the videodisc will become a significant electronic teaching tool in higher education. Accessible by a computer keypad, it can carry both still and moving pictures. It can serve as a slide holder or as a carrier of standard video. It can call up single slides or retrieve frames from the 54,000 frames of a half-hour video program. Its storage and retrieval capabilities make it likely that through the videodisc students in even the smallest institutions will one day have access to the holdings of the world's major art museums, as well as to vast collections of scientific slides and visual materials. Through it, they will also be able to read dictionary entries, encyclopedia articles, and items from a variety of reference works not readily available. The videodisc is useful for both individual and group uses.

If the claims made by some educational technologists as to the influence on learning of visual aids are sound, more and more colleges and universities will want to have on hand videodiscs programmed to provide visuals that will enhance both courses and textbooks. One instructional technologist identifies three "educational applications appropriate for this versatile medium": (1) as a handy chalkboard, videoplayer, slide/tape projector for a teacher, with the teacher using a keypad to call up visual materials; (2) as a tool for small groups working on assigned or special projects; (3) as teaching tool for the individual that provides tutorials, drill, and simulations.[9]

The communications technologies, especially television, will encourage all colleges and universities to become less cloistered. As is already happening, television will become a window on the wide world for them. Through television, they can share their resources with their communities. They can bring more special services to segments of their communities in need of them, just as now they are delivering educational and training services to special professional and occupational groups.

This is not to say that the higher education world will make use of television or other communications technologies to usher in the learning society in the next century. One would be naive indeed to expect that, but television certainly will give colleges and universities greater opportunities to share their riches with the many willing and able to benefit by them.

Notes

Some of the references in the notes that follow can be located readily only through the ERIC Clearinghouse, a U.S. Department of Education–supported computerized repository of documents relating to all aspects of education and training. Whenever appropriate, therefore, ERIC Document Reproduction Service numbers are supplied for the convenience of readers desirous of following up on sources cited.

Readers can access the ERIC system directly by computer in most college and university libraries. Readers can also obtain hard copy or microfiche prints of documents by writing or calling the ERIC Document Reproduction Service, 3900 Wheeler Avenue, Alexandria, VA 22303, 1-800-227-3742.

INTRODUCTION

1. James Martin, *The Wired City* (Englewood Cliffs, NJ: Prentice-Hall, 1978).

2. Eric Barnow, *The Image Empire, A History of Broadcasting in the United States from 1953* (New York: Oxford University Press, 1970), p. 72.

3. *Educational Television: The Next Ten Years* (Stanford, CA: The Institute for Communication Research, 1962), pp. 11, 12.

4. Judith Murphy and R. Gross, *Learning by Television* (New York: Fund for the Advancement of Education, 1966). ERIC Document Reproduction No. ED 012 622.

5. *Time*, October 20, 1967.

6. "Long Distance Learning Gets an 'A' at Last," *Business Week*, May 9, 1988, 108–11. The statement quoted is by Nicholas Johnson.

7. See Walter Perry, *The Open University* (San Francisco: Jossey-Bass, 1977).

8. Wilbur Schramm et al., *The New Media — Memo to Educational Planners* (Paris: UNESCO Institute for Educational Planning, 1967). See also Schramm, gen'l ed., *New Educational Media in Action*, 3 vols., also published by the UNESCO Institute in the same year.

9. Two useful ones are the following: Delayne Hudspeth and R. Brey, *Instructional Telecommunications: Principles and Applications* (New York: Praeger, 1986) and Charles Feasley, *Serving Learners at a Distance: A Guide to Program Practices* (Washington, DC: Association for the Study of Higher Education and the ERIC Clearinghouse on Higher Education, 1983).

CHAPTER 1

1. This is discussed in Asa Briggs, *The History of Broadcasting in the United Kingdom*, vol. 1 (London: Oxford University Press, 1961).

2. Leslie N. Purdy, "The History of Television and Radio in Continuing Education," in *Reaching New Students Through New Technologies*, ed. L. Purdy (Dubuque, IA: Kendall-Hunt, 1983), p. 29. See also D. N. Wood and D. G. Wylie, *Educational Telecommunications* (Belmont, CA: Wadsworth, 1977).

3. Ibid., p. 29.

4. *A Public Trust. The Report of the Carnegie Commission on the Future of Public Broadcasting* (New York: Bantam Books, 1979), p. 256.

5. Ibid., p. 257.

6. Ibid.

7. *Public Television. A Program for Action* (New York: Harper and Row, 1967), p. 35.

8. Interview in *Forbes Magazine*, October 1, 1968.

9. Robert Carlisle, *College Credit Through TV* (Lincoln, NE: Great Plains Instructional TV Library, 1974), p. viii.

10. For an account of the Toronto experiment, see John A. Lee, *Test Pattern* (Toronto, Canada: University of Toronto Press, 1971).

11. Murphy and Gross, pp. 38–40. See also Purdy, "The History of Television and Radio. . . ."

12. James Zigerell and H. Chausow, *Chicago's TV College: A Fifth Report* (Chicago: City Colleges of Chicago, 1974), p. 15. See also the same authors' "Instructional Television: The Recruiting and Training of Teachers," *Comparative Education*, II (March, 1966), 107–12.

13. Much of the interest in open learning and the external degree was stimulated by the work in the 1970s of the Carnegie Commission on Non-Traditional Learning.

14. See, for example, The Commission on Non-Traditional Study's *Diversity by Design* (San Francisco: Jossey-Bass, 1973) and the Carnegie Commission on Higher Education's *Less Time, More Options: Education Beyond the High School* (New York: Carnegie Commission for the Advancement of Teaching, 1971).

15. Alvin Eurich in his preface to Murphy and Gross.

16. See Zigerell and Chausow, *Chicago's TV College*.

17. Carlisle, pp. 46–53.

18. President's Commission on Instructional Technology, *To Improve Learning* (Washington, DC: U.S. Government Printing Office, 1970), p. 19.

19. Quoted in Zigerell and Chausow, *Chicago's TV College*, pp. 10–11.

CHAPTER 2

1. These are the most common obstacles as reported by P. Hammer and D. Slade in a paper prepared for the Association for the Study of Higher Education: "Removing Barriers to the Participation of Adult Learners in Higher Education." The paper is available through the ERIC Document Reproduction Service: No. ED 203 809.

2. Speeches and papers prepared for the conference were published as *Proceedings of the National Conference on Open Learning in Higher Education* (Lincoln, NE: State University of Nebraska, 1974). These proceedings, looked at in retrospect, are a remarkable document in that they show how experienced administrators, state higher education authorities, and public officials had been swept along by the wave of enthusiasm for open and nontraditional learning. Copies of the document may still be available through Nebraska Educational Television in Lincoln, where publications of the State University of Nebraska and its successor institution, the University of Mid-America, are stored.

3. For those readers interested in nontraditional ways students can earn degrees, the following will be helpful: Frank Newman, *Report on Higher Education* (Washington, DC: U.S. Government Printing Office, 1971); Carnegie Commission on Higher Education, *The Fourth Revolution: Instructional Technology in Higher Education* (New York: McGraw Hill, 1972); K. Patricia Cross, *Adults as Learners* (San Francisco: Jossey Bass, 1972); Samuel Gould, *Diversity by Design* (San Francisco: Jossey Bass, 1973); S. Gould and K. Cross, eds., *Explorations in Non-Traditional Study* (San Francisco: Jossey Bass, 1972); Cyril Houle, *The External Degree* (San Francisco: Jossey Bass, 1973); G. Rumble and K. Harry, *The Distance Teaching Universities* (New York: St. Martin's Press, 1982); D. Sewart et al., *Distance Education: International Perspectives* (New York: St. Martin's Press, 1983).

4. C. Houle, "Foreword to American Edition," in Perry, *The Open University*, p. ix.

5. Ibid., p. 9.

6. The BOU student body has been exhaustively investigated. Here are several studies available in this country: Naomi Mackenzie et al., "Student Demands and Progress at the Open University — The First Eight Years," in Sewart et al., *Distance Education: International Perspectives*; N. Mackenzie et al., *A Degree of Difference: The Open University of the United Kingdom* (New York: Praeger, 1977).

7. Mackenzie, "Student Demand . . . ," p. 193.

8. A. Mellar, *Proceedings of National Conference on Open Learning in Higher Education*, 130–32.

9. A. Hershfield, "The National University Consortium — One Year Later," in Purdy, ed., p. 399.

10. See Donald McNeil, *Plan for an American Open University* (Lincoln, NE: University of Mid-America, 1981). Like other University of Mid-America publications, this document is available through ERIC Document Reproduction Services: No. ED 207 455.

11. For a brief summary of the UMA project and its objectives, the reader is referred to Raymond Lewis, *Meeting Learners' Needs Through Telecommunications* (Washington, DC: American Association for Higher Education, 1983), p. 204. This compendium, sponsored by the now discontinued AAHE Center for Learning and

Telecommunications, which was established by a 1981 grant from the Carnegie Corporation, is a handy reference for anyone interested in reviewing profiles of telecommunications-based teaching projects. If it is to remain useful, however, it must be kept up to date. Also recommended to readers with special interest in adult and distance learning are the following: F. Aversa and D. Forman, "Issues in the Evaluation of Educational Television Programs," and F. Aversa, "Evaluation of Distance Learning Systems: Selected Issues and Findings," in Purdy, ed., pp. 270–79 and pp. 318–30.

12. As reported by Lewis, p. 207.

13. See University of Mid-America, *Final Report: UMA Viewership* (Lincoln, NE: University of Mid-America, 1978).

14. Carol Koffarnus, "The Central Educational Network's Postsecondary Service," in Purdy, ed., p. 355.

15. The Mind Extension University is described in the *Business Week* feature article cited in note 6 to the Introduction.

16. This statement is from the proposal for the project as submitted to the Fund for the Improvement of Postsecondary Education of the U.S. Department of Education. The introduction to the proposal is reprinted by Purdy, ed., pp. 331–36 (R. Millard and G. Davies, "Assessing Long Distance Learning Telecommunications: Politics, Procedures and Standards for Accrediting and State Authorizing Agencies").

17. The Texas policy is reprinted as an appendix in Hudspeth and Brey.

CHAPTER 3

1. The cartoon appeared in *The New Yorker* of June 19, 1988, 31.

2. Leslie Purdy, "The Role of Instructional Design in the Telecourse," in Purdy, ed., p. 84. See also T. W. Pohrte, "Planning and Design Process," in Zigerell, J., ed., *Television in Community and Junior Colleges* (Syracuse, NY: ERIC Clearinghouse on Information Resources, 1980), pp. 25–39.

3. James Zigerell, *A Guide to Telecourses and Their Uses* (Fountain Valley, CA: Coastline Community College, 1986), p. 3.

4. Richard Smith, "Educational Television Is Not Educating," in Purdy, ed., p. 119.

5. Anthony Bates, "Trends in the Use of Audiovisual Media in Distance Education Systems," in Sewart et al., *Distance Education.*

6. See Godwin Chu and W. Schramm, *Learning from Television: What the Research Says*, rev. ed. (Stanford, CA: Institute for Communications Research, 1975): ERIC Document Reproduction Services: No. ED 109 985; and James O'Rourke, "Research on Telecommunications and the Adult Learner," in Zigerell, ed., *Television in Community and Junior Colleges*, 13–21.

7. Paul Duby and D. Giltrow, *Students Enroll in a Model Television Course* (Chicago: City Colleges of Chicago, 1976): ERIC Document Reproduction Services: No. ED 134 172. The authors conducted telephone interviews with home viewers enrolled in a telecourse that combined the slick, documentary-style programs of *Man and Environment*, a Miami-Dade Community College production, with a matching number of low-cost, teacher-hosted programs produced by the Chicago TV College.

8. See Hudspeth and Brey for a nontechnical description of nonprint media employed to support off-campus instructional programs. Chapter 7 is particularly helpful. Another useful discussion can be found in J. Terence Kelly and K. Anandam, "Communicating with Distant Learners," in Purdy, ed., pp. 182–93.

CHAPTER 4

1. "Television Course Operations: Expenses Per Course," a publication available from the PBS Adult Learning Service in Alexandria, Virginia. Another good source of information is K. Munshi, "The Economics of Television," in Purdy, ed. This is a chapter from her study, *Television: Reflections,* originally commissioned by the Corporation for Public Broadcasting for the Station-College Executive Project in Adult Education. Although written in 1980 and focused on open-broadcast television, this is still a useful study of telecourse economics.

2. See T. Utsumi et al., "Global Education for the 21st Century; the GU Consortium," *T.H.E. Journal,* March, 1989, 75–77.

3. See Peter Dirr et al., *Higher Education Utilization Study. Phase I: Final Report* (Washington, DC: Corporation for Public Broadcasting, 1981), and Marilyn Kressel, *Adult Learning and Public Broadcasting* (Washington, DC: American Association of Community and Junior Colleges, 1980).

4. Ronald Brey and C. Grigsby, *Telecourse Student Survey* (Washington, DC: American Association of Community and Junior Colleges, 1984), p. 24.

5. The Annenberg/CPB Project National Narrowcast Service demonstration project was summarized and assessed in a report entitled *National Narrowcast Service Final Report: Executive Summary* (Washington, DC: Annenberg/Corporation for Public Broadcasting Project, 1986).

CHAPTER 5

1. See G. Rumble et al., *The Distance Teaching Universities* and B. Holmberg, *Distance Education: A Survey and Bibliography* (New York: Nichols Publishing Company, 1977).

2. James Zigerell, *Distance Education: An Information Approach to Adult Education* (Columbus, OH: National Center for Research in Vocational Education, 1984), p. 37.

3. The short title of the book by Otto Peters (*Die didaktische Struktur des Fernunterrichts, Untersuchungen zu einer industrialisierten Form des Lehrens und Lernens,* Weinheim: Belz, 1973) can be rendered in English as *The Structure of Distance Education.* See p. 206 for the citation.

4. Executive Summary, *Intermedia* (Washington, DC: Annenberg/Corporation for Public Broadcasting Project, 1988).

5. See Charles Wedemeyer, "Back Door Learning in the Learning Society," in Sewart et al., *Distance Education.* Passage quoted is on p. 129.

6. Some of the enrollment figures cited were published in *ITC News,* the newsletter of the Instructional Telecommunications Consortium, which is

headquartered at the American Association of Community and Junior Colleges in Washington, DC. Others come from the *Coast Communicator,* a newsletter published by Coastline Community College District in Fountain Valley, California. Others come from *Facts About the PBS Adult Learners Service,* distributed by PBS, 1320 Braddock Place, Alexandria, VA 22314.

7. A summary of this report is available at no cost from the Congress of the United States, Office of Technology Assessment, Washington, DC 20510-8025. The complete report (190 pages) can be purchased from the Superintendent of Documents, Government Printing Office, Washington, DC 20402. Quotations are from pp. 5 and 6, respectively, of the Summary.

8. *The Third Wave* (New York: William Morrow, 1980), p. 172.

9. *Faculty Perspectives on the Role of Information Technologies in Academic Instruction* (Washington, DC: Annenberg/Corporation for Public Broadcasting Project, 1985).

10. Ibid.

11. R. Smith, p. 119.

12. Herbert Mitgang, "Public TV Expecting $150 Million Gift," *New York Times,* February 5, 1981, C13.

13. *An Invitation to Explore New Opportunities for Higher Education Through Telecommunications* (Washington, DC: Annenberg/Corporation for Public Broadcasting Project), p. 1.

14. As reported in *ITC News,* Spring 1989.

15. This was reported in the Fall 1989 *Coast Communicator.*

16. Hudspeth and Brey have a detailed description of the Kirkwood telecommunications system, pp. 207–15.

17. A recent description of the CSU-Chico program can be found in R. Meuter and L. Wright, "Telecommunications: CSU Chico," *T.H.E. Journal,* May, 1989, 70–73.

CHAPTER 6

1. Munshi, p. 121.

2. Wilbur Schramm and his associates made early studies of the performance of students taking TV courses. (See note 6 to Chapter 3 above.) See also J. C. Reid and D. MacLennon, *Research in Instructional Television and Film* (Washington, DC: U.S. Office of Education, 1967); W. Schramm, ed., *Abstracts of Research in Instructional Television and Film,* v. 1 (Stanford, CA: Institute for Communications Research, 1964); J. Zigerell and H. Chausow, "Chicago's TV College: Summary of Third-Year Comparisons," in Purdy, ed., pp. 280–82; Dallas County Community College District Center for Telecommunications, "Student Evaluation of Telecourses in the Dallas County Community College District," in Purdy, ed., pp. 308–17.

3. See Perry, *The Open University* and N. McIntosh et al., *A Degree of Difference.*

4. L. Purdy, "Evaluation of Telecourses," in Purdy, ed., p. 268.

5. Zigerell and Chausow, *Chicago's TV College: A Fifth Report,* p. 10.

6. R. Shavelson et al., *Executive Summary: Evaluating Student Outcomes from Telecourses* (Washington, DC: Annenberg/Corporation for Public Broadcasting

Project, 1986).

7. M. Cambre, *A Reappraisal of Instructional Television* (Syracuse, NY: ERIC Clearinghouse on Information Resources, 1987), p. 30.

8. J. O'Rourke in Zigerell, ed., *Television in Community and Junior Colleges,* p. 16.

9. M. Moore, "On a Theory of Independent Study," in Sewart et al., *Distance Education,* p. 16.

10. See J. Coldeway, "Recent Research in Distance Learning" and K. Forsythe, "Learning to Learn," in Daniel et al., *Learning at a Distance* (Edmonton, Alberta, Athabasca University, 1982).

11. D. Giltrow and P. Duby, "Predicting Student Withdrawals in Open Learning Courses," *Educational Technology,* February, 1978, 43–47.

12. M. Hoachlander, *The Ascent of Man: A Multiple of Uses* (Washington, DC: Corporation for Public Broadcasting, 1977).

13. R. White, *Motivational and Social Factors in the Use of Communications Technology for Education,* 1980. Available from ERIC Document Reproduction Services: No. ED 211 043.

CHAPTER 7

1. D. Grossman, "Electronic College Courses: The Professor Must Be In Charge," *Chronicle of Higher Education,* February 11, 1987, 104.

2. Copies of the reports published to date of the Telecourse Student Survey are available from the American Association of Community and Junior Colleges, One Dupont Circle, NW, Washington, DC 20036. A brief history of the Instructional Telecommunications Consortium — *The Instructional Telecommunications Consortium: The First Ten Years* — is also available from the same address.

CHAPTER 8

1. HI-OVIS is the acronym for Higashi-Ikoma Optical Visual Information System, which was tested in the Higashi-Ikoma district of the Nara Prefecture. This system in itself is of little interest to most readers, except in its prefiguring the future, providing costs can be kept manageable. For a fuller description of the system, see J. Zigerell, "If It's Worth Doing, Do It Well," *Community and Junior College Journal,* December/January 1983–84, 41 ff.

2. "Britain's University of the Air, an Interview with Lord Walter Perry of the Open University," *The Futurist,* July–August, 1989, 25–26. Harold Shane of Indiana University was the interviewer.

3. Addressable channels are cable channels programmed specifically for special viewers — for a fee. "Institutional Networks" — I-Nets — link specific sites with an organization or institution, and usually allow for two-way communication. Low-power television is a TV broadcast facility with a weak, or small, signal area. For more information about these technologies and their potential for instruction, readers are referred to Hudspeth and Brey, pp. 195 ff.

4. Cambre, pp. 5–7.

5. The findings of this project are summarized in *Electronic Text and Higher Education: A Summary of Research Findings and Field Experience* (San Diego, CA: San Diego State University Center for Communications, 1988).

6. This is from an address given by George Steiner, a literary critic and intellectual historian, to the International Publishers Association Congress in London in 1989. See "The End of Bookishness?" *Times Literary Supplement*, July 8–14, 1989, 754.

7. *Cultural Literacy: What Every American Needs to Know* (Boston: Houghton Mifflin, 1987), p. 20.

8. F. Norwood, "Recent Developments in Telecommunications Technology," in *Communications Technologies: Their Effect on Adult, Career, and Vocational Education* (Columbus, OH: National Center for Research in Vocational Education, 1982), p. 21.

9. Cambre, p. 49.

Selected Bibliography

Adams, T. "Working with Broadcasters." In *Using Mass Media for Learning,* edited by R. Yarrington. Washington, DC: American Association of Community and Junior Colleges, 1979. (ERIC Document Reproduction Services: No. ED 165 856).

Aversa, F., and Forman, D. "Issues in the Evaluation of Television Programs." In *Reaching New Students Through New Technologies,* edited by L. Purdy. Dubuque, IA: Kendall-Hunt, 1983.

Bates, A. "Trends in the Use of Audiovisual Media in Distance Education Systems." In *Distance Education: International Perspectives,* edited by D. Sewart, D. Keegan, and B. Holmberg. New York: St. Martin's Press, 1983.

Beaty, S. "Forming College Television Consortia." In *Using Mass Media for Learning,* edited by R. Yarrington. Washington, DC: American Association of Community and Junior Colleges, 1979. (ERIC Document Reproduction Services: No. ED 165 856).

Brock, D. "Promise and Partnership: Public Television and Higher Education." In *Reaching New Students through New Technologies,* edited by L. Purdy. Dubuque, IA: Kendall-Hunt, 1983.

Carnegie Commission on the Future of Public Broadcasting. *A Public Trust.* New York: Bantam Books, 1979.

Channell, K., and Parker, J. "West Virginia's HEITV: A Grassroots Approach to Telecourse Utilization." In *Reaching New Students through New Technologies,* edited by L. Purdy. Dubuque, IA: Kendall-Hunt, 1983.

Clennell, S., Peters, J., and Sewart, D. "Teaching for the Open University." In *Distance Education: International Perspectives,* edited by D. Sewart, D. Keegan, and B. Holmberg. New York: St. Martin's Press, 1983.

Coldeway, D. "Recent Research in Distance Learning." In *Learning at a Distance: A World Perspective,* edited by J. Daniel, M. Stroud, and J. Thompson. Edmonton, Alberta: Athabasca University, 1982. (ERIC Document Reproduction Services: No. ED 222 635).

Corporation for Public Broadcasting. *Higher Education Utilization Study: Technical Report.* Washington, DC: Corporation for Public Broadcasting, 1979. (ERIC Document Reproduction Services: No. ED 187 342).

Craig, J. "Britain's Open University: Text, Telly, and Tutor." *Change* 12 (October 1980): 43–48. (ERIC No. EJ 234 580).

Dallas County Community College. *ITV Close-Up: The First Six Years.* Dallas, TX: Dallas County Community College District, 1979. (ERIC Document Reproduction Services: No. ED 171 361).

Eldridge, J. "New Dimensions in Distant Learning." *Training and Development Journal* 36 (October 1982): 42–44, 46–47. (ERIC No. EJ 267 944).

Erickson, C., and Chausow, H. *Chicago's TV College: Final Report of a Three Year Experiment.* Chicago: City Colleges of Chicago, 1960. (ERIC Document Reproduction Services: No. ED 021 442).

Feasley, C. *Serving Learners at a Distance: A Guide to Program Practices.* ASHE-ERIC Higher Education Research Report no. 5. Washington, DC: Association for the Study of Higher Education; and ERIC Clearinghouse on Higher Education, 1983. (ERIC Document Reproduction Services: No. ED 238 350).

Forsythe, K. "Learning to Learn." In *Learning at a Distance: A World Perspective,* edited by J. Daniel, M. Stroud, and J. Thompson. Edmonton, Alberta: Athabasca University, 1982. (ERIC Document Reproduction Services: No. ED 222 635).

Giltrow, D., and Duby, P. "Predicting Student Withdrawals in Open Learning Courses." *Educational Technology* 18 (February 1978): 43–47. (ERIC No. EJ 178 054).

Green Chair Group. Predicting Distant Education in the Year 2001. Final Report. Washington, DC: Green Chair Group, National Home Study Council, 1982. (ERIC Document Reproduction Services: No. ED 213 927).

Gripp, T. "Telecourses Have Designs on You." *Technological Horizons in Education Journal* (April 1977): 18–19.

Gross, R. "Instructional Technology — For D Students and Doctorates." In *Planning for Higher Education*. New York: Educational Facilities Laboratory, 1975.

Grossman, L. "Coming Together — Public Television and Higher Education." In *Reaching New Students through New Technologies*, edited by L. Purdy. Dubuque, IA: Kendall-Hunt, 1983.

Hobbs, T. "Consortium Uses of Telecourse Materials in Florida." In *Reaching New Students through New Technologies*, edited by L. Purdy. Dubuque, IA: Kendall-Hunt, 1983.

Holmberg, B. "Guided Didactic Conversation in Distance Education." In *Distance Education: International Perspectives*, edited by D. Sewart, D. Keegan, and B. Holmberg. New York: St. Martin's Press, 1983.

Killian, J. R., Jr., et al. *Public Television. A Program for Action. Report and Recommendations of the Carnegie Commission on Educational Television*. New York: Carnegie Corporation, 1967.

Luskin, B., and Zigerell, J. "Community Colleges in Forefront of Telecourse Development." *Community and Junior College Journal* 48 (March 1978): 8–9, 44–45. (ERIC No. EJ 179 609).

McIntosh, N., Woodley, A., and Morrison, V. "Student Demands and Progress at the Open University — The First Eight Years." In *Distance Education: International Perspectives*, edited by D. Sewart, D. Keegan, and B. Holmberg. New York: St. Martin's Press, 1983.

Meuter, R., Wright, L., and Urbanowicz, C. "Closed-Circuit Educational Television (ITFS) in Northeastern California." In *Reaching New Students through New Technologies*, edited by L. Purdy. Dubuque, IA: Kendall-Hunt, 1983.

Mirkin, B. "Vo-Tech TV OK, But Accept No Substitutes for Teachers." *Community and Junior College Journal* 53 (October 1982): 36–37. (ERIC No. EJ 268 727).

Mittelstet, S. "Telecourse Design, Development, and Evaluation." In *Using Mass Media for Learning*, edited by R. Yarrington. Washington, DC: American Association of Community and Junior Colleges, 1979. (ERIC Document Reproduction Services: No. ED 165 856).

Mount, G., and Walters, S. "Traditional versus Televised Introductional Methods for Introductory Psychology." In *Reaching New Students through New Technologies*, edited by L. Purdy. Dubuque, IA: Kendall-Hunt, 1983.

National Narrowcast Service Demonstration Project. Unpublished paper. Washington, DC: Public Broadcasting Service, 1983.

Nebraska Videodisc Group Newsletter. Lincoln, NE: Great Plains Instructional Television Library, 1983.

Norwood, F. "Recent Developments in Telecommunications Technology." In *Communications Technologies: Their Effect on Adult, Career, and Vocational Education,* edited by N. M. Singer. Information Series no. 244. Columbus: ERIC Clearinghouse on Adult, Career, and Vocational Education, The National Center for Research in Vocational Education, The Ohio State University, 1982. (ERIC Document Reproduction Services: No. ED 220 726).

NUTN News. Stillwater: National University Teleconferencing Network Coordination Office, Oklahoma State University, 1984.

Perry, W. *Teaching and Learning at a Distance: The Experience of Britain's Open University.* Occasional Papers in Continuing Education, No. 15. Vancouver: Centre for Continuing Education, University of British Columbia, 1978. (ERIC Document Reproduction Services: No. ED 162 171).

Potter, G. "Satellite-based Distance Education: Canadian Experiences." Paper presented at the 7th Annual Conference of the SIETAR, Vancouver, BC, March 11–15, 1981. (ERIC Document Reproduction Services: No. ED 206 267).

Project ALLTEL. *Joint Statement of the Accreditation, Authorization, and Legal Task Forces on Assessing Long Distance Learning via Telecommunications.* Washington, DC: Project ALLTEL, 1983.

Purdy, L. *Telecourse Students: How Well Do They Learn?* Fountain Valley, CA: Office of Institutional Research, Coastline Community College, 1978. (ERIC Document Reproduction Services: No. ED 154 851).

_____."The History of Television and Radio in Continuing Education." In *Reaching New Students through New Technologies,* edited by L. Purdy. Dubuque, IA: Kendall-Hunt, 1983.

Purdy, L., and Icenogle, D. *Classic Theatre: The Humanities in Drama: A Television Course for Credit. Final Research Report.* Costa Mesa, CA: Coast Community College District, 1976. (ERIC Document Reproduction Services: No. ED 133 028).

Reid, J., and MacLennan, D. *Research in Instructional Television and Film; Summaries of Studies.* Washington, DC: Office of Education, U.S. Department of Health, Education, and Welfare, 1967.

Rhines, C. *The Maryland College of the Air: A Focused Analysis.* Baltimore: Essex Community College, 1977.

Rumble, G., and Harry, K., eds. *The Distance Teaching Universities.* New York: St. Martin's Press, 1982.

Sewart, D. "Distance Teaching: A Contradiction in Terms?" In *Distance Education: International Perspectives*, edited by D. Sewart, D. Keegan, and B. Holmberg. New York: St. Martin's Press, 1983.

Sewart, D., Keegan, D., and Holmberg, B., eds. *Distance Education: International Perspectives*. New York: St. Martin's Press, 1983.

Singer, N., ed. *Communications Technologies: Their Effect on Adult, Career, and Vocational Education*. Information Series no. 244. Columbus: ERIC Clearinghouse on Adult, Career, and Vocational Education, The National Center for Research in Vocational Education, The Ohio State University, 1982. (ERIC Document Reproduction Services: No. ED 220 726).

Tickton, S. G., ed. *To Improve Learning: An Evaluation of Instructional Technology*, vol. 1. New York: R. R. Bowker Co., 1970.

Toffler, A. *The Third Wave*. New York: William Morrow and Company, 1980.

University of Mid-America. *Final Report: UMA Viewership Study*. Lincoln, NE: University of Mid-America, 1978.

Use of a Newspaper as a Distance Teaching Medium: A Case Study. Unesco Surveys and Studies. Montreal: College Marie-Victorin; and Paris: Unesco, 1983. (ERIC Document Reproduction Services: No. ED 240 327).

Walker, D. "Tight Budgets and 'Socialistic' Image Plague Britain's Open University." *Chronicle of Higher Education*, March 28, 1984, pp. 1, 33.

Waniewicz, I. "Adult Learners: Who Are They, Why and Where Do They Learn?" In *Learning at a Distance: A World Perspective*, edited by J. Daniel, M. Stroud, and J. Thompson. Edmonton, Alberta: Athabasca University, 1982. (ERIC Document Reproduction Services: No. ED 222 635).

Waters, G. "Learning from the Open University: The Limits of Telecommunications." In *Reaching New Students through New Technologies*, edited by L. Purdy. Dubuque, IA: Kendall-Hunt, 1983.

Wedemeyer, C. "Back Door Learning in the Learning Society." In *Distance Education: International Perspectives*, edited by D. Sewart, D. Keegan, and B. Holmberg. New York: St. Martin's Press, 1983.

Weinstock, R. "Chicago TV College Twenty Years Old and Still Innovating." In *Planning for Higher Education*. New York: Educational Facilities Laboratory, April 1975.

Wood, D., and Wylie, D. *Educational Telecommunications*. Belmont, CA: Wadsworth, 1977.

Yeoell, B. "An Interactive Instructional Television Project." In *Reaching New Students through New Technologies,* edited by L. Purdy. Dubuque, IA: Kendall-Hunt, 1983.

Young, E. "Training Via Satellite." In *Proceedings of the Fourth National Conference on Communications Technology in Education and Training.* Silver Spring, MD: Information Dynamics, 1982.

Zigerell, J. "Universities without Walls and with No Illusions." *Educational Television* 3 (October 1971): 17–18, 28. (ERIC No. EJ 046 846).

_____."A Brief Historical Sketch." In *Using Mass Media for Learning,* edited by R. Yarrington. Washington, DC: American Association of Community and Junior Colleges, 1979. (ERIC Document Reproduction Services: No. ED 165 856).

_____."Consortia — A Growing Trend in Educational Programming." in *Reaching New Students through New Technologies,* edited by L. Purdy. Dubuque, IA: Kendall-Hunt, 1983.

Index

ABOUT THE AUTHOR

JAMES ZIGERELL holds degrees from Loyola University of Chicago and the University of Chicago, having received from the latter institution a Ph.D. in English language and literature. After his discharge from the Army at the end of World War II, he joined the faculty of Wright College of the City Colleges of Chicago, where he taught English and humanities. In 1957, he was invited to present a course in English composition on open television. This experience convinced him of the virtues of television as a medium for direct instruction, and, in 1962, when offered the opportunity, he became a member of the administrative staff of Chicago's TV College, eventually becoming director of televised instruction for the City Colleges of Chicago.

Dr. Zigerell has served as a consultant on the uses of television for instructional purposes to the American Association of Community and Junior Colleges, the National Endowment for the Humanities, various colleges and universities, Japan's University of the Air, and the Italian Television Network. He is the author of numerous articles and monographs on uses of television in higher education.